ECLECTIC
WICCA

A Guide for the Modern Witch

Mandi See

Eclectic Wicca: A Guide for the Modern Witch

Library of Congress Cataloging-in-Publication number:
ISBN: (print) 978-1-63353-483-4
BISAC category code REL118000, RELIGION / Wicca

Printed in the United States of America

An ye Harm None,
Do What Ye Will

I dedicate this book to two of the most incredible people in my life, neither of whom got to see it be released. To attempt to explain to you the importance and value of them to my life would be a failure, as I know I wouldn't do them and their stories justice. But I want you to know that without them I wouldn't be close to the person I am now.

My Dad, Peter See, who bought me my first cauldron.

My Gran, Edna Jones, who forever confused Paganism with Veganism. Both taught, in their own ways, the importance of following your heart, even if other people tell you you are doing wrong.

I am eternally grateful to you both and hope I can continue to spread your message. Love you with all my heart.

Contents

Introduction

Have you ever wanted to wave a magic wand and discover you were the proud owner of an omnipresent power that could shape your life in ways you thought impossible? We all have. I am sorry to inform you it doesn't work that way. As much as we all long to receive a parchment envelope with green swirling letters delivered to us personally by an uncommonly obedient owl—that can only mean you have finally been accepted to the most elusive school of all time—it doesn't make it any more likely. What I write for you here, dear friends, is not only very real but also a possibility for every single person who chooses to live this way. Though I have no goblins, flying broomsticks, or noble professors to offer you, I do have a gift to give: this book. As you turn the pages, you will discover Wicca, Magick, and Fairy Dust is not always what it seems in the world you may know. But if you take my hand and follow me down the rabbit hole, I can show you a new world, where you can manifest the life you always dreamed of using only the power of your own passion and intent—and you never have to worry about getting squished by a troll.

Wicca is the religion of modern witchcraft popularised in the 1950s. It falls under the umbrella term of Paganism, so you may often hear Wiccans refer to themselves as Pagan, although Paganism itself is not a religion. The origins of Wicca are inspired by pre-Christian beliefs from when the many parts of Europe still followed the old ways. As a result, many confuse Wicca for a pre-Christian religion, which it is not, though it is strongly based on several.

For many years, Wiccans and witches alike hid away in the shadows and did not publicly advertise their beliefs or practices for fear of being singled out (or worse). Today it is a widely accepted religion—many schools, universities, and work establishments recognize Wicca and its religious holidays, as do many prisons and hospitals.

The desire to master the direction we choose to take in life finds all of us at a different time. Some struggle year after year to lay the concrete foundations of who it is they wish to be. Others are pleasantly visited by a glistening epiphany—for no apparent reason—with the greatest of ease. You may be in the garden the first time you truly connect with nature, hands deep in soil with the incandescent sun smiling down upon your face. Or you may be camping high on a clifftop under the radiant, resplendent moon, listening to the powerful waves of the ocean crash against the rocks like lost ships in a storm. Though this is not the way for everyone, some will connect with nature at the most unlikely of times: whilst in a cluttered office cubicle, enjoying their weekly ritual of watering a cactus, or during a visit to the dentist, distracting themselves with the colours from the glorious tropical fish tank. One way or another, this desire finds us and we are faced with those difficult questions...

Where am I going?
What do I want?
Why do I want it?

These questions are often surrounded by a sinking feeling of self-doubt, but I tell you friends: these questions are not for the faint-hearted. The fact that you are even brave enough to investigate means you are more adventurous and courageous than most.

Those who do not ask never receive.

The choice to follow a path of spiritual enlightenment is not quite like choosing a film for date night, nor is it as straightforward as selecting lowlight colours for your autumn hairstyle. However, it isn't altogether as complex as you may think either. Spirituality is a very broad concept that allows for a lot of wiggle room. In general, it suggests a connection with something bigger than yourself, but the details are negotiable and left open to interpretation. Many people consider themselves to be spiritual without ever committing to follow one specific religion or belief system. In this book, I intend to satisfy your desire to appreciate and comprehend Wicca by illuminating the eclectic form that many practitioners today choose to adopt for their craft. If you have studied any form of Wicca before, you may have discovered the many traditions there are within this journey. It certainly isn't a one-size-fits-all faith (many rarely are). Unlike many Wiccan authors who seek to share the traditional old ways of Wicca that are still valued highly today, I intend to cut into that pie and supply you with a customized slice.

The etymology of the word "eclectic" presents us with synonymous terms such as "selective." I use the word "eclectic" because I choose or pick from various traditions, as you will pick and choose what it is that works for you. There are very few solid rules that must be followed in Wicca, and the ones that stand are basic and simple, put in place purely to disassociate Wiccans from those of similar practices who may potentially wish to cause harm to others or use their knowledge recklessly. I often explain eclectic Wicca and its nature to my clients with a musical analogy. Some people love opera, and why wouldn't they? It is fantastic. They will listen only to opera music night after night, and it fills them with ceaseless bliss. Others love rock, and others love pop. Around the world, individuals at every second are creating playlists upon playlists of their favourite music. But what if you weren't satisfied with just one genre? What if you did love opera but not all opera? What if you liked some opera, but you also liked hip hop and folk music? Then what? You'd create a mixed playlist, also known as an eclectic playlist. Well, faith can be very similar. Some people can read one document or rule book and be completely satisfied, and that is tremendous, but others aren't as pleased with the structure available for one reason or another. They want to create their own spiritual customs. Traditional or eclectic, Wicca is Wicca.

Many Wiccans study in a group, which is referred to as a coven. However, I have always studied as a solitary practitioner. Though not impossible, it is less likely for covens to practice eclectic Wicca, as it can be difficult for all of the members to agree on what is considered important enough to the group to be classed as faith and what should be left to an individual's way of life. So you may find that most eclectic Wiccans and witches are those who practice their faith alone. I have chosen to write this book as a representation of my personal path as a solitary Wiccan witch, meaning that I practice alone and customize my faith alone, so this text will be suitable for everyone. Whether your beliefs are religious or scientifically based, I am sure you will find something here to relate to. Certain aspects of my faith—such as Deity worship—and ways in which I perform my practice have been adjusted so that they are more beneficial to you. The last thing I desire is for you to think it's my way or the highway. In actual fact, it's your way or bore-way.

You will not find much in the way of the history of Wicca in this book. This is not that it is unvalued— quite the opposite actually. But I find personal study to be so important that I felt it more beneficial to you to research history on your own time. Use this text much more like a handbook for the here and now. Following the eclectic way, the information I find exciting about the history of Wicca may not appeal to you at all and the parts that are not in my highest interest may be your favourite.

At the end of each chapter, you will find an exercise. These are designed to help you create your own custom-designed version of Wicca that works solely for you. You may find people who have similar beliefs, but it is very rare to find an eclectic practitioner who shares entirely the same views. I cannot stress enough that you do not have to approach a spiritual journey with fear of "doing it wrong." It is literally impossible to get the connection you have to something bigger than yourself wrong. Will it change over time? I would think so. Will you have exactly the same beliefs for the rest of your life? I highly doubt it. I have been Wiccan for eighteen years, but my beliefs within Wicca have evolved too many times to count. To stand still and never move forward goes against the universe, whatever you believe. If we were meant to stay put, we'd have been given roots like trees. Humans are a busy species with busy jobs, busy lives, and busy minds. I would advise you to find yourself a notebook to both access throughout this book for the exercises and look back on in years to come. It is almost shocking to me when I look back to the early 2000s and see how different my beliefs were to how they are today. I hope they will continue to evolve for as long as I am here.

Now, even though I have included as much information as I can in this book for the beginner eclectic practitioner, I urge you to use the other resources you have available to you to further your study. I know what you're thinking: more books? Not necessarily. It is true, some of us just love to read—if books had calories I would be the size of a house—but others aren't too keen. And though I clearly value printed text as a writer, it is not the be-all and end-all of your study. When it comes to a nature-based faith, nothing in the world can beat going outside. Nothing can compare to walking barefoot on dewy grass or having soil under your finger nails, connecting with the very source that houses every creation ever known to man and even more. What on Earth can teach you more than the Earth itself?

Primitive tribes learned to worship not from books or houses or religion, but from the world around them. They woke up every day to see the sun's lustrous rising and fell asleep under the cool protection of the moon's coruscating face. They watched the lunar cycle from waxing to full to waning again. They watched their surroundings change before their eyes: the soil that homed their foods and the rain that fed the plants. Day after day, they studied the changes of the world's wonders. And what did they do? They worshiped. It is in our nature as human beings to be grateful. Early men didn't want more—they wanted to survive. No one ever went into a cave, laid down their club, pulled back their matted hair, and sighed in agitation that their favourite app was updating and they didn't have enough wireless internet connection. They were grateful for what they had, and the grateful say thank you. All across the world, as they were not able to communicate with one another from place to place, they worshipped in their own way.

There is not anyone, no matter how studied, that can teach you more about your own spirituality than the universe. Taking on a new eclectic lifestyle is as simple as deciding that you wish to do so. However, turning that eclectic lifestyle into eclectic Wicca is a little more complicated. That is why I am here to help you on your journey. I hope that you will enjoy my book and use it as a guide. I hope over time, you will discover many other resources beneficial to your spiritual growth. If you only take one concept from this book with you, then please let it be this one.

Eclectic Wicca is one of the most personal religions to follow. There is no doing it right or wrong, and no one can tell you how you should or should not do it. However, that does not mean that no one will try.

You must keep this truth solid and protected in your core and never let anyone steal it away from you: we are all individual human beings, all programmed differently. Some people eat meat and others do not, but neither is wrong. Some people can't help but find themselves heavily intoxicated by the rush of playing a sport, while others find nothing more pleasurable than an afternoon in bed with a cup of tea and their favourite film. We are all totally different, so it is impossible to find a one-size-fits-all solution when it comes to spirituality. This is your path and journey. You and only you have the right to claim it. You can call it what you wish, speak of it how you wish, wear it publicly, or keep it private. There are many ways to reach the top of a mountain. Here in this text, I am going to share some options.

There are very few real rules to follow in eclectic Wicca, and the ones that are in practice are the simple few that all Wiccans follow. Your practice may look remarkably like Wicca on the surface, but only those who follow the rules can truly claim the title of Wiccan for themselves.

You need not follow them all—you need not follow any—but you get to choose now. Look upon these pages as a recipe book for spirituality. Some things may leave a less than desired tang. Others you may have never even heard of before, but you will be drawn to sprinkle them on top of your own ideas to see if they bring a more exciting taste.

Never forget that your spirituality belongs to you and it always will.

Picking Up
Your Broom

THE MIND

Part One

Who Are the Witches?

B efore you can take your broomstick for a test drive, there are some basics we need to cover. In chapter one, you will find a basic overview of the most important things you will need to know before starting your journey. This will serve as your golden ticket as we head out of the station. It is important for you to remember that this book's focus is eclectic Wicca. Remember that most can be customised and designed to suit you, your needs, your likes and dislikes. Very few things are set in stone, and that is the beauty of the faith. It is absolutely, without omission, yours and yours alone.

What Is Wicca?

Wicca is the fastest-growing spiritual practice in the United States of America and in Europe. I believe that is because those who follow Wicca and use it can see physical evidence that it actually works. In a nutshell, Wicca does what it says on the tin. There is no putting your faith into elements of creation that you cannot see, feel, or touch. There is no dependence on anyone but yourself to create your own reality and live in the world you desire to live in. You need not even leave the comfort of your own home to study, practice, and master the art that is Wicca.

You do not have to follow a hierarchy or be told "the right way" to worship and practice your personal beliefs. You finally get to experience, speak to, and hear back from the divinity within yourself and the universe. It's a way of finally opening up your eyes and seeing the truly sacred in existence, not just in certain places but absolutely everywhere in the world. It's a way to practice and live true in your faith with every breath you take, and the most rewarding thing is you don't have to listen to anyone but yourself. Wicca is that a pathway to the divine.

Many say that Wicca is not about believing something in particular but about experiencing what is actually right in front of you. There is no element of blind faith in Wicca where you have to trust really hard that something exists somewhere despite the fact that you know you will never ever have that idea confirmed completely. Wicca is about experiencing the divine within yourself and the universe. Having a genuine and undeniable connection. When I was very young, I had a friend that told me she wasn't religious because she didn't believe in anything she couldn't see. I accepted her views as she accepted mine, and we got along just fine. She stumbled one day when she realised she had never seen a dinosaur or the solar system in a fathomable way to the human mind. There were too many things she knew existed despite never actually having seen them for herself. My young friend was not believing in the solar system, but experiencing it first hand from the first-person perspective of a human being living on the planet earth.

She wasn't certain about what each and every planet looked like, what stars were entirely, or the shapes, sizes and speeds at which everything moved. She could research to her hearts content but would still only be left with beliefs based on what others had said and recorded. Instead, she was happy to simply experience the solar system for what she personally could see to be ultimate truth. Wicca is a faith based on the truth of the experience. Much like gravity, you do not believe it—you know it exists because you experience it every second of the day. But that doesn't mean you completely understand

Wicca is about experiencing the divine within yourself

all concepts of it or how it came to exist originally. The journey of Wicca lies in the adventure of discovery: the studies, the observations, the lessons. No one graduates from Wicca. There is no base, intermediate, or high level Wiccan. All followers are equal. The only difference is the number of years living with their eyes wide open and experiencing reality for what it truly is.

Unlike a lot of religions, it's highly encouraged for you to question the universe and what you are being told is true. It helps you grow spiritually and mentally. Wicca urges you to challenge the divinity inside of you and out in the universe. It permits you to try and find the hidden camera or who's pulling the strings of puppetry. Wiccans crave to learn and they know truth is all things. Know thyself to know what you truly believe from the bottom of your heart based on real experiences. Trust thyself to trust every experience you have, and be brave enough to stand by it despite what today's society tells you is or isn't impossible.

What Is a Witch?

One of the most common questions I get asked is: what is a witch? There are so many mystical, strange, and confusing rumours that surround the topic, not to mention a certain level of stigma that is still associated with the term today. A witch is a practitioner of the craft of Magick. You may find that, until this moment in time, you have associated the term "witch" with a pointy hat, broomstick, and green skin. Am I close? Well, I am sorry to destroy the fantasy, but it is something quite different altogether. I often wear a hat to keep my head warm, and my skin only turns green when I wear cheap jewellery. As for a broom, I much prefer vacuum cleaners.

Many people today are still scared of witches. This fear stems from many years ago when the Puritans associated witchcraft with the devil, and anyone accused of practicing witchcraft would more often than not meet a very unpleasant end. In truth, most people ruthlessly killed as witches had nothing to do with the craft at all. Often congregations would cry witch if they took distaste to a certain member or family. Women who spoke up or whose opinions differed from those of a man were also condemned to death as a witch. Once a victim had been labelled a witch, there was very little they could actually do to save their lives. Often, they were asked to provide names of other witches and heavily tortured with grotesque devices until a name should leave their lips. Sometimes, innocent people were accused in this way not through malice but just because prisoners were being tortured to give up names of their "fellow witches" and they sometimes obliged to avoid further pain and torture. All who fell prey were labelled as being in league with the Devil. If they did nothing, they would die; if they acted out, they would be killed for disrespecting the Church.

In Wicca, there is no belief in the Devil at all—there is no belief in Hell or in Heaven. So not only is Wicca not associated with the Devil, it is a religion that does not recognise the existence of Satan at all. A Wiccan witch can be defined as a nature-loving human of any gender who includes the practice of the craft in their lives. They acknowledge the divinity within the universe and within themselves. They acknowledge the changing seasons and the wheel of the year. Wicca is a religion of which its followers are witches. However, not all witches follow Wicca.

You may find yourself wondering: where are all these witches I speak of? Where can you find one? Where can you see one? How can you meet a real witch? The chances are, my friend, you have met thousands. We do not look or act a certain way. We do not have special costumes or wear all black to locate each other in public forums. I can all but guarantee someone at your local supermarket is a Wiccan, someone on the local hospital staff, someone in the care home where your friend's grandmother lives. Wiccans are everywhere, and just like you and I they blend into society easily. This is not a disguise. This just is. Wicca is a religion like any other, but instead of using houses of worship, we worship in our gardens, in forests, and in mountains. Instead of reading from one particular rule book we follow basic rules and write our own books, known as Books of Shadows, where we detail our most proud and personal practices.

There is a witch stereotype that we all wear black and skulk around, and I am sure there are witches who look that way. But there are also millions of members of other religions who do the same. To assume a Wiccan has a certain look is to assume all Christians dress in sandals and robes. Another stereotype is that we are all hippies—we smell of incense and cannabis, wear paisley organic clothing, and protest animal cruelty as proud vegans. Again, it is very possible that some Wiccan witches do this—I know a few myself—but that is certainly not all of us. I know Wiccan hairdressers, solicitors, book makers, archaeologists, postal delivery service workers, police officers, exotic dancers, and tree surgeons. Wiccan witches do not fit into a neat little box with a bow on top, just as no one else does. When you find yourself hunting for a witch and desiring to find one, you may find it more useful simply to ask.

Witchcraft is a pre-Christian indigenous religion of the British Isles and the Celtic countries which included Ireland, France, Germany, and Northern Italy. It can be called a religion, as it is actively practiced by a group of people, and it can also be called a spiritual path because it is actively practiced by the individual.

The Natural World

Nature, within Wicca, is classed as a sacred home. The Earth is honoured as a Goddess: as Gaia, Mother Earth, Mother Nature, and by many other names. The Earth creates and houses all life, not just the human kind, and provides us with the resources we need to exist. When we destroy the natural world, we destroy ourselves, our heritage, our ancestry, and our future.

Some Wiccans believe that all living things (including stars, planets, humans, animals, and plants) have a spirit of some type. Many Wiccan rituals deal with bringing harmony and healing to nature. As a direct result of this, a vast majority of Wiccans share a great concern for the environment. Many Wiccans believe the universe is our creator, and yet it exists inside of us all. When we damage ourselves, we chip away at the universal divine source, too.

Many celebrate the gendered and sexual polarity of nature. For example, the fertilizing rain is one manifestation of the male principle; the nurturing Earth symbolizes the female. Wicca is a very peaceful, harmonious, and balanced religion that promotes oneness with the divine in which all exists. There is a deep appreciation and awe in watching the morning sunrise, the moonlight piercing through the branches of the bare winter trees, and the dew on freshly cut grass. To truly love nature, one must truly love themselves and vice versa. If all exists within the universe and the universe exists within ourselves, then we cannot live harmoniously with Gaia if we are at each other's throats or our own. Self-love is taken seriously within the faith because it is believed that unless you can grow to understand, accept, and appreciate the divine within yourself, you will not fully appreciate it outside of yourself. What would be the point of loving the environment and destroying yourself? The same could be said for loving yourself and destroying your environment.

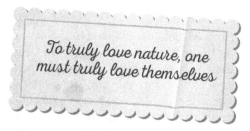

To truly love nature, one must truly love themselves

Nature is the embodiment of the sacred divine. It is the cloak the Goddess wears to shield herself from the cold, the carpet the God walks on as he takes his throne, the bed the Goddess lies on to bear her child, and the grave the God lies in to rest. The natural world weeps spiritual wisdom globally. By working in harmony with nature and learning from nature, holding our rituals along the lunar cycle, and celebrating our joyous sabbat occasions with the cycle of the sun in the wheel of the year, we actually grow naturally. Our consciousness develops. Our connection to the source of the divine—the source of all energy—deepens, and we understand so much more about the world and ourselves as a result.

Divination

Divination is one of the best ways a Wiccan can pay attention to the messages that the universal divine sends to help guide you along your way. It is a way of engaging or conversing with the God and Goddess, and you will find that almost every indigenous culture uses some form of divination. The method of divining is entirely the choice of the witch, and you need not restrict yourself to just one form of divining. Commonly, Wiccans are associated with runes, pendulums, Tarot cards, oracle cards, palm reading, tea leaves, scrying, astrology and so many more. You can even create your own ways. Divination is not so much about how you communicate, but how you learn to interpret the messages you receive. It is a way to truly see that the universe, just like you and I, is a conscious, interactive life source. It has awareness and is awake. The divine is an energy just waiting to be tapped into by all that exist within the universe.

When you cast a spell and you find yourself unhappy or disappointed with the results, it may be because the timing was off when you cast it, or that the desire you had in the present moment of casting did not harmoniously align with the plan set out for you. If you were to use divination before casting the spell, you would receive a message allowing you to understand this and guiding you in a more suitable direction for your highest good.

There are many ways to use divination, some very common like the ones listed below and some extremely uncommon. These are the most commonly practised forms of divination within Wicca.

Glossary

ASTROLOGY is divination using celestial bodies such as the sun, moon, planets, and stars.

CARTOMANCY is fortune telling using cards such as the Tarot.

CLAIRAUDIENCE is "clear hearing" of divinatory information. Parapsychologists generally regard it as a form of extrasensory perception.

CLAIRVOYANCE is "clear seeing" of divinatory information. Parapsychologists generally regard it as a form of extrasensory perception.

CRYSTALLOMANCY is divination through crystal-gazing.

DOWSING or **DIVINING RODS** are methods of divination where a forked stick is used to locate water or precious minerals.
NUMEROLOGY is the interpretation of numbers, dates, and the number value of letters.

OCULOMANCY is divination from a person's eye.
PALMISTRY is a broad field of divination and interpretation of the lines and structure of the hand.

PRECOGNITION is an inner knowledge or sense of future events.

PSYCHOMETRY is the faculty of gaining impressions from a physical object and its history.

SCIOMANCY is divination using a spirit guide, a method generally employed by channelers.

TASSEOGRAPHY is the reading of tea leaves that remain in a tea cup once the beverage has been drunk.

SCRYING is a general term for divination using a crystal, mirrors, bowls of water, ink, or flames to induce visions.

The Divine View

The view of the divine within Wicca is generally theistic and tends to include a Goddess and a God. The theme of polarity is common in Wicca, especially represented with gender, often emphasised as total opposites yet equal in every way. There are certain types of Wicca that only worship the Goddess or the God rather than regarding them as equally important parts of worship. Some Wiccans are polytheists and choose to worships many different Gods and Goddesses that come from one or several different Pagan pantheons of belief. There are Wiccans who are both polytheistic and duotheistic. Many will honour, respect, and converse with several different deities whilst choosing to only worship one God and one Goddess. There is no hard rule that says how exactly your worship must take place or who it is you must worship. Many Wiccans will worship many Deities at different times throughout their lives, depending on the situations they find themselves in and the circumstances they are working with. Some Wiccans simply view the universe as the overall divine source and, to avoid confusion, break that term down into female and male attributes, referring to them as "God" and "Goddess," meaning that it has polarity within itself and can be best described in the knowledge we hold as masculine and feminine.

Unlike many belief systems you may have come across in your life so far, eclectic Wicca allows you to paint your own canvas. This may seem strange and lacking structure, but it is in fact quite the opposite. Every second you exist, you change, grow, and develop. Of course, it goes quite unnoticed on such a small scale, but who amongst us can say we are the same now as we were this time ten years ago, five years ago, or even this time last year? Every experience we have moulds us in one way or another: every death, every birth, every relationship, every breakup. But it isn't just the big things. After one workout at home using full water bottles as weights, your body has started changing, even though you cannot see it on the outside. Every time you eat a bite of food, you change. Every conversation, every idea or thought that pops into your head, sculpts you for the rest of your life with or without your permission. Some changes are very subtle, and some are glaringly obvious to all. It is very hard, if not impossible, to find one size that fits all in a world where our technology is out of date before we learn how to use it properly, in an existence where we have such radically different opportunities, laws, and lives depending on which part of the world we travel to.

Eclectic Wicca allows you to paint your own canvas

Many of us have faith and desire a connection with Gaia, Mother Earth, but we simply don't wish to be told which way we can and cannot converse with her. Some religions of our planet created special houses for their worship, and I think many will agree when I praise the beauty of the sanctuaries they create. But the Wiccan's house is the Earth itself. No building is necessary to commune with the nature that exists within and around us. Wiccans often prefer the freedom of intimate associations with the Moon or Sun as opposed to a statue, but that doesn't mean Wiccans have no structure at all.

There is much freedom in the nature of the craft. This means that no one witch will fall into a stereotypical, structured way of worship, belief, and practice. Many witches belong to traditions within Wicca, but this does not mean they all believe the same things. A tradition is simply the way in which you choose to practice your craft, but your practice is yours alone, and your connection to nature, the universe, the Deities, and all that comes with that will always be customised for your truth.

Unlike following football here in the United Kingdom, connecting to a Deity is not like picking your local team to support. A Greek man or woman might find themselves connected to the Deities of the Greek pantheon, like Aphrodite and Zeus. However, they may find they connect better to a Roman pantheon, Celtic, Egyptian, and so on. No one need follow a pantheon of Deities simply because it is connected to their homeland, though this may be what fuels their personal connection.

I myself, born and bred in the heart of England, find deep connections to many Norse, Roman, Egyptian, Greek, and occasionally Celtic Deities. I have not travelled to all of these places, nor do I have family connections to them all. I cannot explain what it is that pulls me to the Deities I have connected with thus far on my journey. There is no rhyme or reason, but the connection is ever strong and true within my heart and soul.

Some will follow one God or one Goddess. Some will follow a God and Goddess. And some, like myself, will follow and worship multiple versions of the God and Goddess under different names from different pantheons. They are all a representation of the universe within my belief, and so they are all one divine energy. But some Wiccans choose to worship and express that worship with a name, multiple names, or multiple pantheon choices of names per God and Goddess.

Traditional Wicca

There are many traditions within Wicca just like with any other religion. The basic rules are followed in the same way, but the practices are acted out and performed differently. The connection to the divine may be similar, but the worship could be different. Or the worship could be similar, but the divine connection different. Traditions are handed down from generation to generation, witch to witch, in books or online, in covens, in open circles—pretty much any way you can imagine. Long gone are the days of whispers in the shadowy blanket of nightfall. Today's traditions are known as ways to celebrate your faith and the God and Goddess with basic guidelines that have been shared over time and greatly modified to adapt to our modern way of living.

The traditions known today span much of the world.

Gardnerian Wicca was introduced in England in the 1950s by the very famous Gerald Gardner, who felt the old religion should not wither into nothingness but be rejoiced for the beautiful system that it once was.

The Alexandrian tradition was founded in England in the 1960s by Alex Sanders and is said to be a modified Gardnerian Wicca.

Celtic Wicca blends the joys of the Celtic and Druid pantheons with Gardnerian ritual Magick.

British Traditional Wicca is a mixture of Celtic and Gardnerian beliefs.

Dianic Wicca, originally formed in western Europe, is a tradition that focusses on the Goddess and feminism within the craft.

Seax-Wicca was founded by Raymond Buckland in 1973. It is a Saxon-based tradition that did not break the oath of the Gardnerian tradition.

Those are just a few of the many traditions you will discover along the way. Clearly, many find clarity, value, and pleasure in their guidelines. However, there is another tradition—or rather, a non-tradition— known as eclectic Wicca. The practitioners study many belief systems and apply what they believe is best to their own craft, and in doing so, create their own custom-designed structure.

Nothing can be considered wrong as long as the Wiccan Rede and other basic rules are followed, though you may discover certain traditionalists along the way who would say that is not the case. Like with many faiths, you will find that some cannot help but believe their way to be the only way, and will tell whomever will listen. But Wicca is not a faith that focusses on conversion. There is no desire to convert people from any other religion to follow yours. In fact, the mutual respect for and acceptance of all beliefs is part of what makes Wicca such a beautiful path to follow.

The Wiccan Rede

There are very few actual rules you must follow to be Wiccan, but the ones set in place are important all the same. The first of the Wiccan Laws is known as the Wiccan Rede. The Rede is a statement that provides the most basic of laws within Wicca: harm no one and do as you will.

Bide ye Wiccan laws ye must,
in perfect love and perfect trust
Live ye must and let to live,
fairly take and fairly give
Form the circle thrice about,
to keep unwelcome spirits out
To bind the spell well every time,
let the spell be spake in rhyme
Soft of eye and light of touch,
speak ye little, listen much
Deosil go by the waxing moon,
sing and dance the Wiccan rune
Widdershins go by the waning moon,
chanting out the baleful tune
When the Lady's moon is new,
kiss the hand to her times two
When the moon rides at Her peak,
then the heart's desire seek
Heed the north wind's mighty gale,
lock the door and trim the sail
When the wind comes from the south,
love will kiss thee on the mouth
When the wind blows from the west,
departed souls will have no rest
When the wind blows from the east,
expect the new and set the feast
Nine woods in the cauldron go,
burn them quick and burn them slow
Elder be the Lady's tree,
burn it not or cursed you'll be
When the wheel begins to turn,
soon the Beltane fires will burn
When the wheel has turned to Yule,
light the log the Horned One rules
Heed ye flower, bush and tree,
by the Lady blessed be
Where the rippling waters flow,
cast a stone and the truth you'll know
When you have and hold a need,
hearken not to others' greed

With a fool no season spend,
nor be counted as his friend
Merry meet and merry part,
bright the cheeks and warm the heart
Mind the threefold law ye should,
three times bad and three times good
When misfortune is anow,
wear the star upon thy brow
True in love you must ever be,
lest thy love be false to thee
These eight words the Wiccan Rede fulfill,
An Ye Harm None, Do What Ye Will

The Rule of Three

Like karma—the sum of a person's actions in this
and previous states of existence that is viewed as
deciding their fate in future existences—Wicca has a
rule based around your behaviour. Unlike karma, you
do not find yourself nervously awaiting your results
upon reincarnation. Instead, you instantaneously find
out the price of your actions under the Law of Return,
which is also known commonly as the Rule of Three or
Threefold Law.

There are many variations of the phrasing of the
Threefold Law, but they all promote the same thing.

When you take a resource, even with good intentions,
there will be repercussions. What you put out into the
world will be what is returned to you. Many follow the
concept of the Law of Attraction with the Threefold
Law: whatever energies you eject into the world will
be what you receive back. Now the Rule of Three often
gets a bit confusing. Many people follow the belief that
whatever they do will be returned to them three times
as powerfully. So following that theory, if you are kind

and caring you will receive kind and caring back three times as much as you gift, and if you are cruel you will receive your cruelty back three times as powerfully. However, it isn't quite that simple. The Rule of Three refers to mind, body, and spirit. Whatever you put out will affect your life, your future, your growth, your wellness, your health in your mind (mentally), in your body (physically), and in your spirit (you guessed it: spiritually). The Rule of Three is mentioned within the Wiccan Rede.

> *Ever Mind the Rule Of Three, Three Times Your Acts Return To Thee This Lesson Well, Thou Must Learn Thou Only Gets What Thee Dost Earn*

When you pay someone a compliment or act with kindness and genuinely mean it, you are rewarded in mind body, and spirit. Your body is filled with warmth and love, and you promote your health. Your mind is filled with joy and your spirit grows ever closer to that of divinity. When you act wickedly towards a person and shout aggressively, you are punished in mind, body and spirit. When your body is filled with rage, your mind becomes agitated and potentially, upon looking back, guilty, which in turn affects your body with the sinking feeling from mistreating others and disappointing yourself. Your spirit sinks and decreases its connection, which carries you away from living harmoniously in your truth with the universe.

The Thirteen Principles of Belief

The catalyst for bringing witchcraft out of the closet and opening its doors to a wider audience was the passing of the Fraudulent Mediums Act of 1951. The Fraudulent Mediums Act was a law in England and Wales which prohibited a person from claiming to be a psychic, medium, or other spiritualist while attempting to deceive and make money from the deception. It repealed the Witchcraft Act of 1735, and it was in turn repealed on 26 May 2008 by new Consumer Protection Regulations following an EU directive targeting unfair sales and marketing practices. The passing of the Fraudulent Mediums Act gave the individual freedom to practice so long as their activities harmed no one, hence the Wiccan Rede. And sticking to the subject of rules and regulations... In April 1974, the Council of American Witches adopted a set of Principles of Wiccan Belief.

The Council of American Witches finds it necessary to define modern witchcraft in terms of the American experience and needs. We are not bound by traditions from other times and other cultures, and owe no allegiance to any person or power greater than the Divinity manifest through our own beings.

As American Witches, we welcome and respect all life-affirming teachings and traditions, and seek to learn from all and to share our learning within our Council.

It is in this spirit of welcome and cooperation that we adopt these few principles of Wiccan belief. In seeking to be inclusive, we do not wish to open ourselves to the destruction of our group by those on self-serving power trips, or to philosophies and practices contradictory to these principles. In seeking to exclude those whose ways are contradictory to ours, we do not want to deny

participation with us to any who are sincerely interested in our knowledge and beliefs, regardless of race, colour, sex, age, national or cultural origin, or sexual preference. We therefore ask only that those who seek to identify with us accept these few basic principles.

1. We practice rites to attune ourselves with the rhythms of life that are marked by the phases of the Moon, the Seasonal Quarters and Cross Quarters.

2. We realize that our intelligence gives us a special responsibility towards our environment. We strive to live in harmony with Nature, to achieve a balance in the fulfillment of our lives.

3. We acknowledge a power that is greater than that which is apparent to the average person. This power is sometimes labelled "supernatural," but we understand that it lies within that which is a natural potential to all.

4. We see the Creative Power as a manifestation of the masculine and feminine, and that this same Power lies in all people and functions through the interaction of the masculine and feminine. We do not value one above the other, knowing that they are supportive to each other. We value sex as pleasure and the embodiment of life.

5. We recognize both the outer worlds and the inner psychological world, and realize that the interaction of the two is the basis of magical exercises. We neglect neither of these, seeing both as a necessity for our fulfillment.

6. We do not recognize any authoritarian hierarchy, but honour those that teach, respect those that share knowledge and wisdom, and acknowledge those who have the courage to lead.

7. We see religion, wisdom and magic as being united, not only in the way we view the world but also in the way we live in it. This philosophy of life is identified as "Witchcraft - the Wiccan Way".

8. Giving oneself the title of "Witch" does not make you a Witch, neither does heredity, nor the collection of titles, degrees or initiations. A Witch seeks to control the forces within him/herself, thus making it possible to live wisely and well, in harmony with Nature and not harming others.

9. We believe in the affirmation and fulfillment of life as a continuation of evolution, as well as the development of consciousness which gives a deeper meaning to the Universe that we know and an understanding of our personal role within it.

10. Our only animosity towards Christianity, or any other religion or philosophy of life, is to the extent that they claim to "be the only way" and have thusly sought to deny the freedom of choice by suppressing other ways of religious practice and systems of belief.

11. As Witches, we are not threatened by debates on the history and origins of the Craft, nor the legitimacy of the various aspects of the traditions that surround Wicca. We are concerned with our present and our future.

12. We do not accept the idea of absolute evil, nor do we worship the entity known as "Satan" or the "Devil" as defined by the Christian Tradition. We do not seek power through the suffering of others, and therefore do not accept that personal benefit can be derived by denial to another.

13. We believe that we should seek within Nature that which is contributory to our health and well-being.

The Wheel of the Year

A large part of Wicca is celebrating your connection to the universe or the God and Goddess. There are eight spiritual festivals throughout the year known as the Wiccan Sabbats. These special days mark special times in nature and reflect what is happening in nature at the time. As an eclectic Wiccan, the way in which you celebrate can be as traditional or untraditional as you choose.

Not every Wiccan has the chance to celebrate the festivals on the specific day due to work or other commitments. However, more and more companies, schools, and universities recognise these religious holidays by the day. I have never had a problem booking time off work for a religious holiday.

When you research these holidays further, you will discover an array of costumes, practices, and traditions around how, when, and why to practice. Some of them are very glamourous and others very basic, but the important thing to remember is that you can choose for yourself how you practice. Getting very dressed up for the Solstices, Equinoxes, and the Cross-Quarter Sabbats may be more refined. Or, like me, you may pick the ones you personally enjoy the most to go all out and celebrate the others lower-key. I know Wiccans who celebrate entirely alone, quietly at home, and others who go to a festival for each one and make quite the day and night of it. Stonehenge is an extremely popular venue for the Solstices and I myself have enjoyed many a sabbat in Glastonbury, England.

The sabbats follow the annual cycle of the sun, so these festivals celebrate the journey of the God in most traditions. The Goddess is forever present within his journey and becomes especially worshipped toward the darker part of the year. She is generally worshipped as she is nurturing the seed of the God inside her pregnant belly. The Goddess is more often associated with the moon and Lunar cycle, so she is celebrated throughout each month.

Some Wiccans believe a sabbat is the perfect time for rituals and spell work, whereas others stay away from it on these days and use their time and energy entirely for celebrating.

Many Wiccans will set up an altar dedicated to the God and Goddess during the time of the sabbat. It is common to decorate the altar with the colours present in nature at the time and with naturally fallen treasures found outside in nature at this time. It is not always possible to find naturally fallen objects, such as flowers, so what many Wiccans choose to do is to ask permission of the earth, plant, soil etc., to take the item and leave an offering in return. This may be seeds to grow new life, or maybe birdseed to feed those outdoors. The main point of the offering is to aid life, so it must be something that in no way damages or potentially harms the earth or its inhabitants, so do not use anything that will pollute or cannot biodegrade.

The Wiccan sabbats include:

Samhain - 31st October (pronounced Sow-in):

The Wheel of the Year is seen to begin at Samhain, which is also known as Hallowe'en or All Hallows Eve. This is the Celtic New Year, when the passage between the worlds of life and death stands open. Samhain is a festival of the dead, when Pagans remember those who have gone before and acknowledge the mystery of death. As Pagans, we celebrate death as a part of life.

Yule - 21st December (archaic form Geola, pronounced Yula):

Yule is the time of the winter solstice when the sun child is reborn, an image of the return of all new life born through the love of the Gods. The Norse had a God Ullr, and within the Northern Tradition, Yule is regarded as the New Year. The reason a lot of Wiccans celebrate this sabbat is to mark the God's rebirth from the Goddess. The sun is a symbol of the God, and as the God grows up, the sunlight stays in the sky longer.

Imbolc - 2nd February:

Imbolc, also called Oimelc and Candlemas, celebrates the awakening of the land and the growing power of the sun. The Goddess has now rested and makes her appearance again as the young maiden. The God is now rapidly growing but is still a child. Often, the Goddess is venerated in her aspect as the Virgin of Light, and her altar is decked with snowdrops, the heralds of spring.

Spring Equinox - 21st March:

Now night and day stand equal. The sun grows in power and the land begins to bloom. By Spring Equinox, the powers of the gathering year are equal to the darkness of winter and death. For many Pagans, the youthful God with his hunting call leads the way in dance and celebration. Others dedicate this time to Eostre, the Anglo-Saxon Goddess of fertility. As the earth becomes fertile, so do the God and the Goddess. Both are now young adults and the courtship has begun. Just as the seedlings sprout to life, so does the womb of the Goddess.

Beltane - 30th April:

The powers of light and new life now dance and move through all creation. Beltane is the day where the Goddess and God Unite. The crops have been planted, and the life inside the Goddess is starting to show. The Wheel continues to turn. Spring gives way to Summer's first full bloom, and Pagans celebrate Beltane with maypole dances symbolizing the mystery of the sacred marriage between the Goddess and God.

Midsummer - 21st June:

At summer solstice is the festival of Midsummer, sometimes called Litha. The God in his light aspect is at the height of his power and is crowned Lord of Light. It is a time of plenty and celebration. The God is at full strength during this time, and the Goddess's pregnancy grows larger as the crops continue to grow along with the Goddess.

Lughnasadh - 1st August (pronounced Loo-nassa):

Lughnasadh, otherwise called Lammas, is the time of the corn harvest. It is when Pagans reap those things they have sown and when they celebrate the fruits of the mystery of Nature. At Lughnasadh, Pagans give thanks for the bounty of the Goddess as Queen of the Land. The God starts to grow weaker as the child within the Goddess grows bigger and stronger. The Goddess starts to mourn the coming loss of her husband but is comforted in the fact that he will be re-born from her soon.

Autumn Equinox - 21 September:

Day and night stand hand-in-hand as equals. As the shadows lengthen, Pagans see the darker faces of the God and Goddess. For many Pagans, this rite honours old age and the approach of Winter. This is the time when the God prepares for death and his time to rest.

Samhain - 31st October:

The Wheel turns and returns to Samhain, the festival of the dead, when we face the Gods in their most glorious forms. This is not a time of fear, but rather a time to understand more deeply that life and death are part of a sacred whole. The God has now died, and the Goddess mourns him, turning the world cold. Lore says that the western gate opens to allow spirits to cross and join us in celebrations for the night, or to allow those to cross over and be with the God as he rests and awaits his re-birth at Yule.

The Lunar Cycle

The lunar cycle marks sacred times in nature also. Unlike the Wheel of the Year that follows the sun and reflective times in nature, this cycle follows the moon at sacred times known as esbats, occasions that happen much more often. Many Wiccans perform rituals at one of these times or all of them.

They will often conduct their spell work depending on the lunar cycle, as it is believed there are better times to attract certain things into, or banish them from, their lives.

The Lunar Esbats include:

THE FULL MOON: used for Banishing, Protection, and Divination workings, and also for Planning, Releasing, and working Backward in Time. It can be said that the best Full Moon magic has a seven-day window. These days include the three days before the Full Moon, the Night of the Full Moon, and the three days after the Full Moon. Sometimes, the results of the Magick take a Full Moon cycle in order to be completed.

THE NEW MOON: used for Personal Growth, Healing, and Blessing of a Personal Venture. The results from a New Moon should be seen by the start of the next Full Moon.

THE WAXING MOON: a time for Attraction Magick for anything which you wish to gain such as Prosperity, Wellness, or New Love.

THE WANING MOON: a time for Banishing and Rejecting things from our lives, whether they be Negative Emotions, Bad Habits, Diseases, or Ailments.

THE DARK MOON: the period three days before the New Moon. Traditionally, this is a time for Rest. No Magick will be performed at this time. Deep Meditation and Vision Questing can be performed at this time, but not for Magical Purposes. However, Hecate rules over this time. If you need her Magick, now is the time to call upon it.

There are Thirteen Full Moons, each with an Individual Name.

The New Moon

The Waxing Moon

The Waning Moon

The Full Moon

January – Wolf Moon	August–Wyrt
February–Storm Moon	(Green Plant) Moon
March–Chaste Moon	September–Barley Moon
April–Seed Moon	October–Blood Moon
May–Hare Moon	November–Snow Moon
June–Dyad (Pair) Moon	December–Oak Moon
July–Mead Moon	Variable–Blue Moon

The Elements

The Four Elements are commonly spoken of as Earth, Air, Fire, and Water. However, there is another element that many find difficult to define or describe, and because of this it is often left out of conversation. The Fifth Element—or the First, depending on how you see it—is called Ether or Spirit. It is the most elusive and ethereal of the all and cannot be categorised or explained accurately, as everyone has a different view, connection, and idea of exactly what it is. We all know the look, sound, taste, and sensation of the other Elements, but no one can agree entirely on Spirit.

The Element of Earth is the one that is most closely linked with our dimension and physical world and, obviously, is the densest of all of the Elements. The Air Element is a delicate balance between the Four Elements that make up our universe. The Fire Element is closely associated with the masculinity of the sun, the speed and force. It gives life and governs passion and respect. The Water Element trickles deep within our subconscious. It reflects our emotions, our love, and our dreams. It influences moods and responds to that which happens on the surface and beneath.

We use these Elements both in belief and in life, in magickal ritual and in daily practice. Over time so many of these foreign concepts will become second nature, and you won't have to make the conscious effort to include them into your life. You will find them settling quite nicely at the foundation.

Let's Talk Magick - Glossary

Within Wicca and many witchcraft belief systems, there are certain words and phrases used that those who do not follow the faith may not understand without some explanation. If any words or phrases in this book should crop up that you are unsure of in nature, refer to this glossary to help decipher the language of magickal practitioners. You may find you know more of them than you realised.

Air – one of the Four Magickal Elements

Akasha – the Fifth Element, also called Spirit or Ether

Altar – table or flat surface used during rituals to hold ritual tools, books, etc.

Amulet – a magickally-charged item, often worn around the neck for protection

Animism – the spiritual belief that everything in nature, animate and inanimate, possesses a soul

Ankh – Ancient Egyptian symbol representing life and rebirth that is similar to, but not the same as, crux ansata

Aquarius – the eleventh sign of the Zodiac, ruling from January 21 – February 19, and an Air sign ruled by the planet Uranus

Aries – the first sign of the Zodiac, ruling from March 21 – April 20, and a Fire sign ruled by the planet Mars

Astral body – representation of person or things found in astral plane

Astral plane – a kind of dimension composed of energy

Astral projection – an out-of-body experience, usually induced through trance

Athame – small, double-edged ritual dagger, usually black-handled, used to draw Circles and direct energy

Aura – an energy field surrounding all living things

Balefire – a sacred outdoor fire burned by some Wiccan at certain Sabbats

Banish – to drive away or release a spirit or energy

B.C.E. – Before Common Era; an alternate dating system corresponding to B.C.

Beltane – Sabbat held on May 1st; also known as May Day, May Eve, Rood Day, Roodmas, and Walpurgisnacht

Besom – a magickal broom

Binding – a spell which generally involves tying knots in cords or a similar action, aimed at restricting energy or actions

Bolline – a small, white-handled knife

Book of Illuminations – alternate name for what is traditionally called Book of Shadows

Book of Light – alternate name for what is traditionally called Book of Shadows

Book of Shadows – a collection of rituals, notes, spells, etc., as well as sometimes a journal of workings

Burning Times – a name given to the Reformation and Inquisition, when the Church actively killed people for practicing "witchcraft"

Cancer – the fourth sign of the Zodiac, ruling from June 22 – July 22, and a Water sign ruled by the Moon

Candlemas – Sabbat held on February 2nd; also known as Imbolg/Imbolc, Oimelc, or Candelaria

Capricorn – the tenth sign of the Zodiac, ruling from December 23 – January 20, and an Earth sign ruled by the planet Saturn

Cauldron – a pot or kettle that is generally used as Goddess symbol

C.E. – Common Era; an alternate dating system corresponding to A.D.

Censer – an incense burner

Ceremonial magick – the art and practice of controlling spirits through force of will, which requires dedication and study

Cernunnos – the Celtic god and often-used name for Wiccan Lord (not universally accepted)

Chakras – seven energy points within the body

Charge of the Goddess – a well-known piece of poetry by Doreen Valiente

Chalice – a special glass/goblet used in rituals

Circle – a magickal construct used in rituals

Cone of power – energy raised and focused by group or individual for magick-working or ritual

Consecration – the act of blessing an object with positive energy

Corn dolly – a human or animal figure fashioned out of a sheaf of corn that is used in spells and as fertility symbol

Coven – a group of people who come together for ritual and study

Craft, The – Witchcraft (also a Masonic term)

Crone – one of the aspects of the Threefold Goddess; the term can also refer to an older, wise woman

Deosil (day-o-sil) – clockwise direction, also known as "sunwise"

Divination – the art of foretelling future events or revealing knowledge through the use of tools (e.g., Tarot, runes, etc.)

Drawing Down the Moon – invoking the Goddess into oneself, usually in a ritual

Dawning Down the Sun – invoking the God into oneself, usually in ritual

Earth – one of the Four Magickal Elements

Eke-name – one's sacred and magickal name

Elements – the five ancient building blocks of the universe – Earth, Air, Water, Fire, Spirit

Enchantment – another word for spell

Esbat – a regular meeting of a Wiccan coven or circle; it sometimes refers to Full or New Moon rituals

Eostre – Spring Equinox Sabbat

Evocation – calling up spirits or other magickal entities

Fetch – a name of one's astral body

Fire – one of the Four Magickal Elements

Gardnerian tradition – the Wiccan tradition which traces unbroken lineage to Gerald Gardner

Gemantria – Hebrew numerical science which consists of adding up the numerical value of a word and comparing it to other words with the same value

Gemini – the third sign of the Zodiac, ruling from May 22 – June 21, and an Air sign ruled by the planet Mercury

God – the male aspect of the paired deities; the Lord

Goddess – the female aspect of the paired deities; the Lady

Goddess worship – a type of pagan faith where the female divinity is the major focus; this concept is not just found in Wicca

Green Man – the representation of the Lord as ruler of the forest

Grimoire – a book containing a collection of spells

Ground/grounding – (the/to) root self in physical world

Hand, projective – the energy-emitting right hand

Hand, receptive – the energy-receiving left hand

Hand fasting – a Wiccan marriage ceremony

High magick – ritual magick that is focused on the spiritual realm

High Priest/HP – male head of a coven; representative of God

High Priestess/HPS – female head of a coven; representative of Goddess

Horned God – generally seen by Wiccans as the male consort of the Goddess; he is a male deity with stag horns rising from his head

Imbolc/Imbolg – the Sabbat held on February 2nd

Incantation – a ritual recitation of a prayer or spell, usually rhymed, to produce a magickal effect

Invocation – calling upon a higher power (deities, Spirit, etc.) for support or assistance

Karma – the force generated by a person's actions thought to determine the nature of one's next incarnation

Lammas – the Sabbat held on August 1st

Left-hand path – the use of magick for selfish gain and/or evil

Leo – the fifth sign of the Zodiac, ruling from July 23 -August 21, and a Fire sign ruled by the Sun

Libra – the seventh sign of the Zodiac, ruling from September 24 – October 23, and an Air sign ruled by the planet Venus

Litha – the Summer Solstice Sabbat

Lingam – a stylized phallic symbol of the masculine cosmic principle

Low magick – green magick, or magick generally focused on the physical

Lughnasadh – the Sabbat held on August 1st

Mabon – Fall Equinox Sabbat

Magick – "The Science and Art of causing Change to occur in conformity with Will" (as defined by A. Crowley)

Maiden – one of the aspects of the Threefold Goddess; the term may also refer to a female assistant to High Priestess in some traditions

Meditation – the act of engaging in quiet contemplation or reflection

Midsummer – Summer Solstice Sabbat

Mother – one of the aspects of the Threefold Goddess

Neo-Paganism – an umbrella term referring to modern-day practices which aim to revive nature religions, Goddess-worship, and/or mystery traditions

New Age – a modern spiritualism movement, followers of which believe that we create our own reality

Numerology – a method of divination that analyses the symbolism of numbers

Old Ones – a name encompassing all gods and goddess

Old Religion – used to refer to Witchcraft, Paganism, and/or Wicca (lots of differing opinions here as to its correctness)

Ostara – Spring Equinox Sabbat

Pagan – a non-Christian, Muslim, or Jew

Pentacle – a five-pointed star that is three-dimensional

Pentagram – a five-pointed star that is two-dimensional

Pisces – the twelfth sign of the Zodiac, ruling from February 20 – March 20, and a Water sign ruled by the planets Jupiter and Neptune

Polytheism – belief in, or worship of, more than one god

Querent – used in divination; the person who asks questions of the reader

Rede/Wiccan Rede – "An it harm none, do what thou will"

Ritual – a religious or magickal ceremony characterized by formalized actions and words

Ritual magick – high magick, or magick focusing on spiritual realm

Runes – a divination tool using symbols carved into wood or stone; the term also refers to symbols and early alphabets

Sabbats – the eight holy days based on the seasons

Sagittarius – the ninth sign of the Zodiac, ruling from November 23 – December 22, and a Fire sign ruled by the planet Jupiter

Samhain – the Sabbat held on October 31st

Scry – to gaze into or at an object with the intent to see future events or distant places

Scorpio – the eighth sign of the Zodiac, ruling from October 24 – November 22, and a Water sign ruled by the planets Mars and Pluto

Skyclad – naked

Solitary – a name given to Wiccans or other pagans who work and worship alone

Spell – a magickal working aimed at changing reality

Spirit – the fifth of the magickal Elements; an animating or vital principle within all living beings

Sympathetic magick – magick which works on the principle that like attracts like; the term also refers to image magick and creative visualisation

Talisman – an object marked with magickal signs that is used for protection or to attract beneficial energy

Tarot cards – a set of 78 cards, 22 Major Arcana and 56 Minor Arcana, used for self-discovery or divination

Taurus – the second sign of the Zodiac, ruling from April 21 – May 21, and an Earth sign ruled by the planet Venus

Theism – the belief in the existence of a god or gods

Threefold-Goddess – the goddess with three changing faces: a Maiden, Mother, and Crone

Threefold Law – the belief that all actions, good or bad, are returned three times over

Tradition – a group of covens sharing a common lineage, rituals, and beliefs

Virgo – the sixth sign of the Zodiac, ruling from August 22 – September 23, and an Earth sign ruled by the planet Mercury

Wand – a ritual tool that is usually made of wood and 21 in length (though this varies a lot today)

Water – one of the Four Magickal Elements

Wheel of the Year – a term used by Wiccans to mean one complete cycle of the year encompassing all eight Sabbats

Wicca – an Earth-Based religion

Wiccan – a follower of Wicca

Wiccaning – a Wiccan birth rite where the Lord and Lady are asked to watch over the baby

Widdershins – counter-clockwise direction

Witch – a practitioner of witchcraft

Witchcraft – the art of spell-casting, focusing mainly on low magick

Yang – a term used in Taoism referring to the active, male, positive principle

Yin – a term used in Taoism referring to the passive, female, negative principle

Yoni – a stylized representation of the female genitalia symbolizing the feminine principle

Yule – Winter Solstice Sabbat

Planting
The Seeds

THE BODY

Part Two

Magick with A "K"

I t may have become apparent to you that I have been spelling the word Magick with a K, and this is not an error. Magick, in the context of witchcraft of Aleister Crowley's Thelema, is a term used to differentiate occult Magick from stage and entertainment magic. It is defined as "the science and art of causing change to occur in conformity with will." Magic is the trickery and illusion you see when a street magician pulls a rabbit from a hat, but Magick is the craft of directing your intent to manifest your truth into reality.

Growing Your Seed of Intent

You will find it hard to achieve anything in life without having true intent behind it. It is impossible to speak if your brain does not intend it to happen, it is impossible to move if those signals are not sent via a chain from head to limb, and Magick works in the same way. Whether you are conducting spell work, ritual, or the simplest of celebratory tasks, with no intent to fuel your desire you are simply speaking, acting, or gesturing for no real reason. Intention is the most powerful tool you can possess as a Wiccan, and it is one that can never be taken away from you. Many Wiccans like to perform spell work at an altar decorated for the specific occasion and perform ritual in a sacred space under the moonlight. However, sometimes life gets in the way. I like to celebrate all of the Sabbats with a ritual of thanks, and I normally do these at home, casting my circle with my altar in the centre with all my tools and comforts surrounding me. However, this is not the only way I have ever achieved rituals.

In the year 2011, I was hospital-bound with a severe case of pancreatitis and there was no hope of returning home for Imbolc, the first Sabbat of the year, which lands on February 2nd. It was the first time I would miss my Sabbat ritual. I had no candles, no altar, no besom or incense, and very little energy to stand from my bed— even if my ritual had been permitted, which is highly unlikely—in the centre of a hospital ward. Instead, I did something that since has become second nature to me: I visualised the entire ritual in my mind. I created my circle, and I called on the elements, spirit guides, and Deities to be present. I silently versed my words of power and gave my gratitude entirely in my mind just after midnight when everyone else was fast asleep. I can honestly tell you that was one of the most powerful rituals I have ever conducted.

The reason this ritual was so powerful was because not having the physical items before me made me focus my intentions twice as much as usual. My altar without intention is simply a coffee table draped in a pretty cloth with statues, flowers, and candles placed on top. Only with my intention does it become the centre point of my circle. My besom is simply a broom, my incense is just a stinky stick, and my words of power are just poetry. Without intention, these items that I spent so many years working hard to get just right were useless. No one will ever stumble across a spell, read it aloud, and accidentally make Magick happen. Without the will of intent, Magick does not exist. Imagine you have the desire to improve your health. In that moment, you purchase yourself a top-of-the-range treadmill. It's the most expensive treadmill in the country, and all of the celebrities have it. It is so high-tech that it has to be specially fitted at your home and set up when delivered. This item is the best health assistance money can buy. But this cannot change your life if you simply own the treadmill. You will soon notice not a lot is happening. You aren't going to feel any fitter or shed any pounds. You aren't breaking any records or even breaking a sweat. Do you know why? Because owning a tool does not create wonders. Using the tool does. And the only way to use the treadmill is with your intent. Only then will you get results.

Reading a spell aloud without intent is simply reciting poetry, smudging your home with sage without intent is simply a way to remove unwanted odours, casting a circle without intent is a quick and easy way to make yourself dizzy and waste your time. Without intent, Magick is simply a fantasy. You will find yourself no further ahead than you once were as a child playing witches in the school yard. Intent is the key ingredient to all magickal workings, and without its presence, the only thing you will create is disappointment and lack of confidence in your own abilities.

Law of Attraction

Now before we get into the nitty gritty of what exactly spell work and ritual are, there are a few key things you must understand. Many Wiccans, though not all, also apply the Law of Attraction to their practice. Simplified, this means what you give is what you attract. Putting out kindness attracts kindness; putting out negativity attracts negativity. When you conduct yourself in a certain way, your energies vibrate on that level, and energies always hunt for a match. For example, you may have found that at particularly difficult times in your life you seem to constantly run into more obstacles, and in more pleasant, uplifting times in your life it feels as if nothing can go wrong.

In more recent years, the scientific concept has been

publicised greatly, and many non-religious members of society also use the Law of Attraction to aid them in their lives. It is now a popular tool for life coaches as well as spiritual gurus.

There is no real trick behind the Law of Attraction. It simply works with your intent like anything else. Many find it useful to meditate on what it is they are trying to invite into their lives as a way of aligning their current energetic vibrations with a positive match. You may have heard the saying: "the rich get richer and the poor get poorer," and I am sure you have experienced that to be the truth when you look into our current society. But have you ever wondered why? I shall tell you. The poor get poorer quite simply because they focus on the lack of what they have. They focus on prosperity always being out of reach. They are obviously doing so in order to attempt to change this cycle, but when you focus on what is out of reach, you attract more out-of-reach energies into your life. The rich however do not focus on the money at all. The rich focus on abundance. They have what it is that they need, and so rather than focus on making more money, they focus on the abundant lifestyle they have grown accustomed to, which aligns their energetic vibrations with abundance and attracts more of it. I do understand how hopeless it seems for a penniless person to focus on abundance when they have very little, but I also understand the benefits of that concept very well, given that I was in that very same situation.

The Law of Attraction is not about tricking the mind into being delusional and relying on fantasies to provide the life you desire. Rather, it is simply about aligning your energetic vibrations with what it is you wish to attract into your life. Everyone has that one friend who is exceptionally unlucky in love. It may even be you. Life has got them down, and they have lost hope in the concept of a happy relationship. Yet they keep half-heartedly entering relationships only to find that the same disappointment and resentment follows them everywhere they go. They are aligned with attracting disappointment and resentment into their relationships because of their previous experiences. The fault lies far from them, but the responsibility to take control of their own actions is not quite so distant. For that person to truly turn things around, they must first acknowledge their part in the cycle and be willing to change it.

Spell work and ritual will only work for you if you are aligning your vibrations with what it is you are trying to attract. We aren't pointing our magickal wands and creating instant gratification. Magick does not work that way. It is not a quick fix. To truly create effective spells that actually work for you, they must be fuelled by the truest of intent and worked by a practitioner who is aligned to their desires.

It is unlikely that you would really want to attempt to work Magick that is not aligned with your desires, which will only result in a disappointment. If you are focussed on negativity, then you cannot bring positivity into your life with Magick. If you managed to achieve anything at all, it would be simply a void where the negativity used to be. If you have a full bucket of water that has dead leaves that have sunk to the bottom and you want to remove the leaves, then the simplest solution would be to pick them out one by one. But in doing so, you will create an overflow in the already full bucket and you will lose some of your water. A better solution would be to add more water until the bucket overflows, carrying all the leaves to the surface and emptying them onto the ground. Instead of picking out the negativity, which means you focus on negativity, focus on filling yourself so full of positivity that there is no room left for the negativity.

Raising Your Vibrational Frequencies

When we go about raising our vibrational frequencies to align without desires, there are certain things we must take into consideration and certain work that needs to be done. The first thing I will suggest is learning to stop resisting that which we feel we do not like. When you resist and push against things you do not like, using the concept of the Law of Attraction, you will simply create more of what it is you despise. Instead, you must simply focus on what it is that you do like. The act of pushing away or resisting means you are focussed on the negativity, and that is what you will feel: like you are constantly fighting to achieve. In return, you will only achieve more negativity.

Being eclectic means you have the ability to pick and choose what aligns with you and you alone. Sometimes you will hear a person make a statement that does not entirely ring true for you, but that does not mean you must disassociate from the entire statement. You can keep hold of the bits that serve your purpose and release those that do not resonate with you.

Consciousness and vibrational frequency go together likes peas and carrots. A low consciousness creates a low vibrational frequency. The perceptions you have are limited, and you can have a tunnel vision. You are unable to comprehend as much due to your ego, which restricts your life force to the universe and divinity. As a result, your intuition will be foggy and your intent will be impure. When your consciousness is high, you have a high vibrational frequency which heightens your perception, allowing you to comprehend much more and actually feel a physical and mental connection to Deity and the universe.

Holding a higher vibrational frequency allows you to radiate a non-judgmental, unconditional love. As a result, you will raise the consciousness of all of those who come into contact with your energy fields (because vibrations need to match).

When you have had an argument with your partner, you can find yourself walking on eggshells so as not to rock the boat any further. You are focussing on the current agitation so as not to cause more. But that means you are also focussing on negativity, and so you are bringing your vibrational frequency down to one which attracts negativity. Instead, you could focus on the forgiveness and moving forward from your argument. This will align you with a higher vibrational frequency and attract positivity into your energy fields. Eventually, in your company, your partner's energy fields will match your own.

I am going to give you some suggestions from quite literally an endless list of things you could do to raise your vibrational frequency.

- **Make conscious positive changes**
- **Use your intuition rather than your ego**
- **Exercise: work out but make sure it is in a way you enjoy**
- **Create and write in a gratitude journal**
- **Music: create yourself an uplifting playlist**
- **Spend time with people or places that have a high frequency**
- **Watch films, videos, or read books that uplift or inspire you**
- **Aromatherapy**
- **Colour therapy**
- **List your blessings and make a gratitude list**

- Smile as often as you can
- Focus energy on what you enjoy
- Give yourself honest and true compliments that you believe
- Allow yourself time to focus entirely on yourself (however long or short a time you can get)
- Spend time in nature, in the garden, in water, in the sun, in the moonlight
- Be kind and help others
- Analyse and question yourself
- Laugh as often as you can
- Dedicate yourself to your happiness

Your vibrational frequency will change continuously, that is why it is important to take conscious action in ensuring it remains higher. Having a low vibrational frequency will not only affect how you feel physically and mentally, but it will also affect how you feel spiritually, which will weaken your connection to the universe and, as a result, your connection to Magick. You will find your practice to be ineffective. To truly work Magick, a lot of self-work is needed, and this is not the type of work you can do just once. To be a successful witch takes constant study and self-development, always moving forward. This means continuously changing it up and challenging yourself. Athletes do not stay in shape by doing the same routine day in, day out for years on end. Eventually, their bodies get used to their workout and they must change it entirely for it to continue working. Being a witch is very similar: it takes a lot of hard work.

Grounding

Grounding is the act of pulling our focus back to our physical dimension. Often, our lives have us so busy, flustered, stressed, and emotionally confused that this can cause us to almost detach from our reality altogether and disappear into a place in our heads where all manner of things can happen. Situations and fears can grow beyond the realms of possibility. Anxieties run wild without their leashes. We can become wildly self-destructive if we stay in this place for too long. To perform effective spell work, we must first be grounded and in our right minds.

When we ground, we allow ourselves to be fully here with our physical bodies by conducting earth or Gaia energies through our root chakra into our physically incarnated perspectives. Like raising your vibrational frequencies, there are far too many ways to ground yourself to list them all, so I have listed some of my personal favourites.

- **Eating food from the earth (any form of vegetable naturally grown without pesticides or chemicals)**
- **Spending time in nature**
- **Meditation outdoors**
- **Surrounding yourself with grounded people and places**
- **Walking barefoot on the earth, the grass, the soil, or the sand**
- **Spending time in water**
- **Visualisation**
- **Deep purposeful breathing**
- **Focusing on your body and how it feels**

- Wearing colours associated with the root chakra or the earth such as reds, browns, blacks and deep greens
- Lying on the ground
- Placing your hands on the ground
- Bringing your attention to the present moment
- Gardening
- Wearing or carrying crystals such as hematite, smokey quartz, red coral, onyx, obsidian, black tourmaline, ruby, garnet, tiger's eye, pyrite, and black opal
- Essential oils
- Sounds, crystals, bowls & drums, and toning
- Guided meditation

If you find yourself ungrounded when it comes to actively practicing Magick or casting, then you may find your focus is not present, which will result in absence of intent.

Meditating

There are many things in life that are beyond our control. However, it is possible to take responsibility for our own states of mind and change them for the better. Despite its popularity in today's society, there are very few people who fully understand what meditation is. Many confuse the term with an act of sitting—rather uncomfortably—cross-legged and making sounds whilst trying to think about absolutely nothing. I think you will be extremely pleased to learn this is not the case.

Meditation is a state of thoughtless awareness; it is not an act of doing something. It is simply an awareness.

"Meditation is a
state of thoughtless
awareness"

We are either in a state of meditation, also known as awareness, or we are not. It is true that some like to sit cross-legged whilst creating sounds to align or ground themselves, but that is not the only way to meditate. Walking barefoot on the grass can be a form of meditation. The key is bringing yourself to the awareness of the present. It is hard to walk barefoot on the grass without being aware of the sensations underfoot. Standing in the rain can also be a form of meditation: counting the raindrops that kiss your skin, combing your hair, washing up. Even pain can form awareness. I think you will find it hard to discover any woman in labour who did not feel fully aware of every sensation in the present moment. However, I certainly would not recommend self-harm as a form of meditation. Not only is it exceptionally dangerous, it goes against the basic Wiccan beliefs.

Another form of meditation is a guided meditation: a soothing voice guides you through visions and sensations and breathing exercises as you listen to and follow the instructions, all bringing you to the present. To conduct any form of Magick, you must have a heightened sense of awareness. This is why meditation, though it does not stem from Wicca, is so highly practiced in most (if not all) traditions.

There are two perspectives within us all: the observer and the experiencer. The experiencer holds the role of ego or body, and the observer holds the role of the soul or the consciousness. Becoming aware of the observer role of your current life experience is also a tool meditation is used for. There are many benefits of meditation including: awareness of self, reducing stress, a newfound appreciation for life, increasing your attention span, increasing your immunity to disease, improving metabolic damage, as well as aids in regulating your sleeping pattern, improving brain function, a deeper sense of connection, and helping you feel overall happiness.

Vision Boards

Vision boards are not entirely a Wiccan concept and are used by many people throughout the world. However, they are fantastic in terms of attracting the vibrational level you desire for the things you wish to achieve into your life. A vision board is a board, poster, or picture of sorts where you list, collage, or put images of what you desire to manifest in your life. You could add things you are working on, such as passing your driving test or getting a new job. The process of creating the board can be done in many ways, and you can make it as magickal or as mundane as you wish. The board should be visible to you every day, hung on a mirror, on the back of the bathroom door, or on the refrigerator—somewhere you will frequently pass. Sometimes you may take time to really study the board and others you will simply see it out of the corner of your eye, but both are valuable to your energetic vibrations. Each time you see your board you are subliminally penetrating your subconscious mind with the things you desire to achieve, which will fill you will more motivation and create natural urges to push for your goals.

Visualisation

Visualisation is the simple act of seeing something and believing it. As children, we all visualise each time we play games. When we play with our dolls, an orange tea towel becomes a warm sandy beach. When we jump stone to stone, the grass is a crocodile swamp. I was first made conscious of visualisation when I was sixteen years old and I went to a performing arts school. At the end of our vocal lesson, we would all lie on the floor as the tutor guided us through beautiful visualisations of flowers blooming before our eyes. In performing arts, the technique of visualisation is key to acting the role you must play. When you need to cry because your character has gone through tragedy, it is very hard to switch on that kind of emotion with nothing to fuel it. But if you can visualise real tragedy in your mind and believe it no matter how illogical it seems, you can tap in to all sorts of emotion and power.

In Wicca, visualisation plays a large role in manifesting your desires into reality. We spoke about the Law of Attraction and how the rich get richer because they focus on abundance. Well, what if you are not rich but wish to focus on abundance as a way to change what it is that you attract? A powerful visualisation can make that mindset a reality and literally change a limited belief system that you have carried your entire life.

The key to visualisation in Wicca is not to focus on what you want and how to get it, but instead to focus on being the type of person you are when you have what it is you desire. Instead of imagining yourself surround by piles of money, which in itself carries a very low vibrational frequency, visualise the type of person you would be if you had abundance: how you would act, the way you would hold yourself.

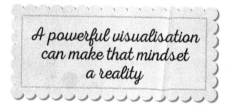

A powerful visualisation can make that mindset a reality

Would you be a kind and moral individual, or would you become cruel and unjust?

We only want to attract things into our lives that align with our highest good. So if you visualise yourself with what you desire and you find you are unhappy with the way you would conduct yourself, then you will have to work on that area of yourself before you can attract what you desire into your life.

Let's say you want to lose weight and you visualise the new you: slim, healthy and full of energy, but something is wrong. You are not happy. You are full of anxiety, and you want to hide yourself away. No matter what you do, you cannot shake the feeling of distaste and self-loathing for your body. What do you do now? You get to work. Start analysing these feelings and converse with this new you in your visualisation. Ask yourself why you feel this way.

What makes you unhappy? What do you feel you are missing? There is a chance that even with your new, slim body you still were not able to shake the feelings and perceptions you carried whilst you felt unhealthy or overweight. Logically, you know you are beautiful inside and out at any size. Logically, you know you are desirable at any size. Logically, you know your true self-worth at any size. But living with cruel perceptions of yourself for such a long time has moulded your perception to be something quite limited and unpleasant.

Only after you have worked through these issues will visualising your new self truly help you attract this desire into your life.

Now I am going to share with you a visualisation technique, and I want you to perform it as you read it for the first time.

Before you is a bowl of lemons: bright yellow, ripe to the touch, aromatic. You can smell the scent of their zesty skin even now. You take the lemon closest to you and give it a little squeeze. It's firm, but it flexes under the power of your fingertips. Place the lemon on your cutting board. With the sharpest knife you own, cut into the lemon. As you slice, the cold and potent juices ooze from its flesh and soak onto your fingers. The dewy centre appears as one half rolls onto its side. You move your hand to your lips, careful not to allow the juice to run down your hand, and lick the bitter liquid off your fingers. Its sharp tang hits your tongue like a flame that cools instantly, and you feel your jaw tighten just below your earlobes.

Did you taste the lemon? If so you have successfully completed a visualisation.

If not, do not worry. You can try the technique over and over as many times as you like. There are also many guided visualisation tracks out there that can help you practice. When you master the art of visualisation, your spiritual practice will benefit immensely. Not only will you be able to align yourself with what it is that you desire, but you will also use visualisation as motivation to achieve your results and as a way to change limited beliefs.

Spell Work

Before you can cast a spell, you need to fully understand what a spell is. There are so many misconceptions in today's world. There is nothing supernatural about a spell or spell casting. For something to exist it must be natural. All supernatural phenomena are considered to be impossible, existing within the third dimensional realm of possibility. However, that in itself is a contradiction. For if something exists, then it is of nature and is, therefore, natural. A spell is not a quick fix or form of instant gratification that comes together with a few fancy rhyming words, a few props, and a mixture in a cauldron that brings whatever your heart desires. That, my friend, is simply impossible.

A spell is a form of prayer. The difference between a spell and the prayers you may be used to hearing is that you are not praying to a Deity outside of yourself to make things simply happen for you because you asked very nicely. With a spell, you are directing your energy with your most honest intentions to either the universe or a Deity(ies) that are both greater than you but that also exist within you. You are asking the place where the universe and your own inner power meet to give you the courage, strength, and abilities needed to accomplish what it is that you are trying to achieve.

The spell work itself is a form of art, a way of reaching the divinity within yourself, finding the gifts you possess, and offering them up to the universe to be directed in the way they are seen fit to serve your purpose (if it is honest and true). You direct your energy—or seeds of intent—out into the universe and use your will to manifest into reality what it is you are trying to grow and achieve. A spell is the act of planting the seed out in the vast garden of the universe. Your intentions are the act of watering and caring for the seed as it sprouts and grows into something beautiful and strong over time.

It is important that you understand you are not casting a spell and simply waiting for the achievement to fall into your lap. You are planting a seed and doing everything in your power to ensure its growth and development. A good example would be an unemployed witch casting a spell to gain money. If you do a spell for money, it is more than likely going to manifest after a lot of hard work on your behalf: updating your CV, hunting for available positions, applying for jobs left, right, and centre. Then, a job will turn up and you will have the ability to earn the money you so desired. You cannot expect to win the lottery if you are too lazy to purchase a ticket. Your achievements are your own and they are something you can be proud of. The universe does not just give you everything you desire in the moment, and it never will. You must participate in your own life and be fully engaged with the process if you expect to achieve anything. The universe will hand you opportunities, but only if you are working hard enough to

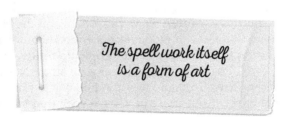

The spell work itself
is a form of art

deserve them and have your eyes open wide enough to see them when they are in front of you.

Spell casting is not as simple as using a vending machine. You cannot just pop in your pennies, choose what you want, and expect your results to fall out of the bottom instantly. The universe is as divinely living as you and I. It is not a machine full of goodies ready to drop when we say our Magick words. It will work with us but not for us. Spells are not forms of manipulating the universe. They are forms of engaging with the universe. An accurate and effective spell requires true and honest intent from your higher self, a high vibrational frequency, a fully grounded practitioner, and gratitude for the partnership of the divine within and outside of yourself.

You must also consider the design of the universe and the potential of destiny within your path. Even when you possess all of the abilities listed, there are still times when a spell does not work. This is not because you did anything wrong, but because there is a grand design. Sometimes what you think you desire in the moment can interfere with the direction you are heading overall, and the seed in the garden of the universe will never flower no matter how lovingly you tend to it. You may apply for many jobs and not even be called for an interview. Why? Did the spell flop? No, it is simply that just around the corner is an opportunity too valuable to waste, and if you had taken a job that had been offered, you may not have had the courage to turn it down and experience what was designed for you instead.

If you revert back to the Wiccan Rede, you will note the last words: "and ye harm none, do what ye will." This refers to harming yourself as well as others and the planet. Something that is a common misconception about Wiccan spell work is that you can make people do things—fall in love with you, for example—but that goes strongly against the Wiccan Rede. To take away the free will of another is a form of harm. You cannot perform a spell that interferes with anyone else's desire and destiny. You can try, but it would not work. If you cast a spell to ensure you landed a specific job, you may be disappointed to discover that your results appear rather differently. But what you must remember is that someone else's destiny is potentially on the line here, too. Someone else may be better, more equipped, and more deserving of that particular job despite the fact that you did a spell.

I often get asked for love spells. Love spells are very possible, indeed, but not necessarily in the way that you may think. Attempting to go against the free will of a human being in order to force them to fall for you is a flop from the start, but love spells are exceedingly effective on yourself. You may cast a spell for self-love and self-acceptance, which often works extremely well and has beautiful results. Or you may cast a spell of true love upon yourself which will aid you in being courageous and open enough to find your true love in life, as many of us struggle with hidden shadows that prevent us from finding such a thing even when it is right in front of our eyes.

You may be thinking: "what is the point in Magick if I have to abide by all of these rules?" Well, the Universal Laws are put in place for a reason, and they are much older than any human ever to have existed. They protect us all. Though you may desire to control another's free will, are you not glad that it is impossible? You never know: if it were possible someone might just do it to you! Spell work provides a purpose just like everything within the craft, but spells are not the be-all and end-all of Magick. Being a Wiccan witch is about much more than just casting spells. Although I won't lie, they are a very appealing aspect of the faith.

How to Cast

A spell is not something that should be rushed into. Many things are taken into account before casting even the simplest of spells. Many consult with the universe first in the form of divination to get an idea of whether or not what they desire to manifest is actually aligned with their highest good (as humans can often have tunnel vision and not see the big picture). If they feel their message indicates the spell is a good idea, then they may then consult the lunar cycle, the time of year, and many other personal connections before they go ahead with their magickal working. Some traditions insist on taking three days and three nights to fully contemplate and weigh up all the potential consequences of casting the spell before making the final decision to go ahead and work the craft. As it is highly unlikely you are aligned with the desire, and that your intent fully supports the hurried action, a spell that is rushed will more than likely fail to manifest. Only when you are completely sure you wish to cast a spell should you move forward.

Be guided by the power of the divine inside and outside of yourself. If you have used a form of divination before you choose to cast, you may find you have been presented with the obvious element in which to use during your spell. Sometimes it may be Earth, the slowest working spell, often used to overcome addiction and commonly used in banishing. It may be Fire, the fastest working spell of all, often used in times of great crisis and detriment to self. Sometimes you may be guided to use a combination of all the Elements, but it is important that you are following that which you are guided to use. A weight-loss spell cannot be achieved with instant results because losing weight takes time. A spell using entirely the Element of Fire will more than likely fail to blossom in this case due to the lack of consideration included in the nature of the working.

There are times when a spell will work but not in the way you intended. There is an element of risk with any spell, though not in terms of danger or disaster when it comes to Wiccan spells. We never attempt to cast anything that would harm or be unethical. However, there can still be undesired results. We do not always cast from the conscious mind, and it sometimes is not our choice. There are times when we will cast a spell with the greatest of intent and discover we have tapped into our unconscious mind and, therefore, our unconscious intent. We all have shadows hidden deep inside of us. Inner thoughts, fears, guilt, desires, resentments, and frustrations are bubbling away at all times. Sometimes, when we least expect it, our spell will work in such a way that reveals an unconscious intention instead, and as a result we learn something quite unknown to us about our inner shadows.

Despite the unexpected and not always pleasant nature of these results, they are entirely crucial to our spiritual journey and understanding of self and they are never an accident. Each spell that ends up this way is a very valuable lesson we must all learn at some point, so be aware when casting that you never know exactly how your spell will work. This is one of the reasons many consult the sacred divine with tools of divination before they cast.

When it comes to asking for exactly what you want, being too specific can come back to bite you. It is always a good idea to leave enough wiggle room for the divine universal energy to express itself. It will never harm you or hand you anything you can't handle, and it will always work in your highest good and align with your current vibrational frequencies. As we said before, you needn't ask for a specific job, as that may not be in your best interest at the time; you simply ask for employment and let the universe align you with results that are the best for you with the bigger picture in mind.

It is important that you realise a spell is not begging and pleading with the God and Goddess to give you what you want. It's simply asking them to work with you in achieving the results you desire.

You could read a spell from a book or website and it could potentially work. But you need to understand that spell work is not like setting up a bookshelf. Reading an instruction manual for one specific bookshelf will not allow you to erect all bookshelves safely and effectively. If you find a spell in a book for healing, then you need to be sure you fully understand exactly for what that spell was written. Was the spell written to heal someone with an illness or an injury? Was the spell written to perform with the sufferer's permission or without? (As performing without permission goes against the patient's free will, this would come under the category of harm.) Was the spell written to perform on yourself as the unwell member or on someone else? Was the spell written for distance healing or in-person? Do you need tools, and if so, what kind and why exactly? It is not wrong to use other people's spells, but they need to be understood entirely.

At all times, you must keep in mind that the universe is a living, existing body. You work with its constant interchanging energy, and work with your own, and allow the universe to work with you. Baking a cake with a friend involves you each having specific roles. Sometimes you will start to whisk only to find you have no skill in the area, and so your friend will take over and show you how. But she will give you back the whisk after a minute or two to ensure you know for next time how to do it alone. Work respectfully with the universe. Do not expect to have everything done for you, and do not expect to run the show entirely alone. A partnership consists of two separate forces merging to create one result.

What Is a Ritual?

The definition of the word "ritual" is: to perform an act in a ceremonial way. Rituals exist everywhere in our lives. When we wake up and brush our teeth, we perform this act ritually. We use the same toothpaste each day which we keep in a specific place, we use the same toothbrush which we also keep in a specific place. We carry out the activity in the same way, which is generally the way we see is most effective to us, and we close the ritual the same way each time by rinsing our mouths, turning off the tap, screwing the lid back onto the mouth wash, and putting all the tools we used away. A Wiccan ritual is very much the same.

A ritual is something we do with a specific purpose in mind. We choose a place to hold our ritual, we gather the tools we intend to use, we open our ritual in a certain way, we perform our ritual and close it in a certain way, and put everything back in its place. The difference between the ritual of brushing our teeth and a Wiccan ritual is...you've guessed it, our intent.

The purpose of the ritual, in a general sense, is to connect our mundane life with our spiritual journey. We create a safe and comfortable place in which we feel we can connect directly to and converse with the God and Goddess or divinity. We can give thanks—or work our craft—here in the ritual we hold, and those around us understand that we are not to be disturbed. Just like when we are brushing our teeth, other adults understand that this is not the best time to attempt to engage with us. We are already busy performing an activity and will not be able to respond and engage with them until with have completed it.

A Christian ritual would be described as visiting a church: a place to connect and reflect with their Lord and father God. As Wiccans do not have Churches or a specific place to visit to connect with the Deities, we cast a circle and perform a ritual which in itself becomes our spiritual house. Sometimes a ritual will be performed outside under the light of the moon, and at others it will be performed in the living room with the furniture pushed back to allow the space you need. Whatever appeals to you and is at your disposal is perfect.

Ritual is a time to balance our higher selves or intuition with our ego state of mind, a place to seek harmony between the conscious and unconscious mind. We dip into the well deep down inside ourselves to infuse our bodies, minds, and spirits with the sacred divine universal energy that allows us to see clearly and gain true and honest perspective in the world and in our lives. We converse with the God and Goddess and receive messages of guidance, love, power, strength, and courage in all we currently are and hope to ever be. We use our time here to meditate and find the stillness, to ground and focus on reality, to contemplate all that is, ever was, and will be. We seek answers for our ongoing questions and find light to illuminate our shadows.

We honour the divine during the times of the sabbats and esbats. We enter ritual gracefully, full of gratitude and respect, and create a sacred space to perform spell work if we choose. In ritual, we share our most private thoughts, desires, feelings, and ideas. Some choose to work fully nude, also known as Skyclad, not in a sexual way but as a way to fully share themselves in their most natural and truest form with the universe.

Performing ritual can be very draining work, so it is important that it be done only when you are truly up to the challenge. If you are unwell or feeling weak due to exhaustion or other reasons, you may find your ritual to be disappointing and the connection you desire to be absent. Even when fully awake and well, you may find the act of ritual can change your energy levels drastically. You may find your energy levels are so high that before closing the ritual, you need to ground yourself and meditate. Or you may find your energy levels are so low that you need to eat and drink something immediately. To ensure that their energy levels are not too drained by the end, many Wiccans include cakes and ale on their altars to eat at a certain point of ritual. As eclectic Wiccans, you can add whatever it is you desire to eat and drink to the altar. The results will be the same. Your concentration and true focus of intent are needed to conduct your ritual, so your energy level must be taken into consideration and managed.

We enter ritual gracefully, full of gratitude and respect

There is no right or wrong way to conduct and perform a ritual as long as you are happy with your choices and decisions, you are feeling content in doing the ritual, and do not feel you are forcing yourself. For your act to be considered a Wiccan ritual, it must follow the Wiccan Rede at all times, and the Threefold Law must be taken into consideration.

How to Perform a Ritual

Casting a circle is one of the most all-encompassing and profound ways of changing your state of consciousness. The act of casting the circle is a way of stepping into the conscious trance to align and connect with the presence of the sacred divinity. The circle is a symbol of the Goddess, as any womb-like representation is, not to mention a symbol of infinity and creation. The moment you cast your circle and stand present inside it, it stops being simply a symbol and becomes an act of invocation in a sphere that envelopes you and fills you with the clarity of what it is to truly converse with the universe. You connect to the sacred inside your circle as if connected by three cords. The cords are deeply connected inside of you to your mind, to your body, and to your spirit. The other ends of those cords are connected to the mind, body, and spirit of the living creation that is the universe. Together, you engage as one whole. You are separate as physical beings but whole and united in the esoteric unknown. It's almost as if you are both plugged into a machine that can transfer information from one to the other and back again.

Within the circle, energy is equally distributed. In many classes in the physical realm here on Earth, a teacher will stand at the head of the class and distribute knowledge to a group of students before them. Within the circle, rather than there being a hierarchy or figurehead that we look upon in awe, we're equal. The universe and the self are one, and so they are equal in power. Inside your circle, you engage with the presence of Deity. So you are receptive, but you are also giving as much as you're getting. You're not silent and passive waiting for something to happen, but you're also not talking continuously. We were given two ears and one mouth because we were designed to listen and learn more than we were to speak and teach. But it's important to remember that we do need to speak or else we wouldn't have been given the ability.

A circle is a boundary of energy. When you cast it, you enter it and you remain inside the circle until you are ready to leave. If for some reason you do need to leave the circle during ritual, you visualize cutting a doorway to leave the circle and you close it behind you. Imagine, if you will, that the circle is full of extreme heat. You have a warm fire blazing inside, and outside of the circle it's snowing so heavily that you can barely see your fingertips in front of you. See the circle as your house. If there were a blizzard, you wouldn't walk outside and leave the door wide open for the heat to escape. Instead, you would close the door securely as you ventured out into the snow, open the door upon your return, and close it behind you. The circle contains the energy within it.

There are certain things you may wish to consider before you perform a ritual.

Firstly, consider what your ritual is for. My rituals tend to be for magickal working or to give thanks. My second step of preparation falls into the more specific, physical realm in a list I always follow:

- **Moon Phase**
- **Astrological Sign**
- **Ritual Bathing (Cleansing of Self)**
- **Clothing/Skyclad**
- **Where & When**
- **Tools and Items**
- **Who You Are Addressing and Connecting With**
- **To Wear Jewelery or Not**

(The last point may seem a tad silly, but some traditional Wiccans will not wear anything inside of the circle that has not been cleansed, consecrated, and charged beforehand.)

So when you intend to cast a circle and perform a ritual, first you must decide where your ritual is going to take place and the amount of space you will need. Most solitary witches cast fairly small circles. You want to ensure you have enough space for your altar and yourself to be present on the inside. I also check to make sure I can stretch out completely, lie down completely, and sit comfortably within the boundaries of space I have set for myself. Before you cast a circle, it is a good idea to use a form of divination you feel comfortable with to ensure it is a good time for you to perform a ritual.

It is always a good idea to make a list of items you want inside of your circle before you begin your ritual. The amount of times I have cast my circle, sat down, and meditated only to realise I have left a crucial tool or a lighter for my candles on the other side of the room is too high to count. Make sure everything you need is present and inside of the space. You may wish to take a cushion or pillow, and maybe even a blanket, inside the circle with you. I have included a copy of my personal list:

- **God and Goddess Candle or Representation**
- **My Working Candle**
- **Headphones, Meditation Music, Music Device**
- **Elemental Representation**
- **Wand or Athame**
- **Besom**
- **Pentacle**
- **Chalice**
- **Libation Bowl**
- **Cakes/Cookies and Drink**
- **Bell**
- **Salt to Make the Circle**
- **Meditation Cushion**
- **Book of Shadows**
- **Lighter**
- **Moon Water**
- **Soil**
- **Incense**

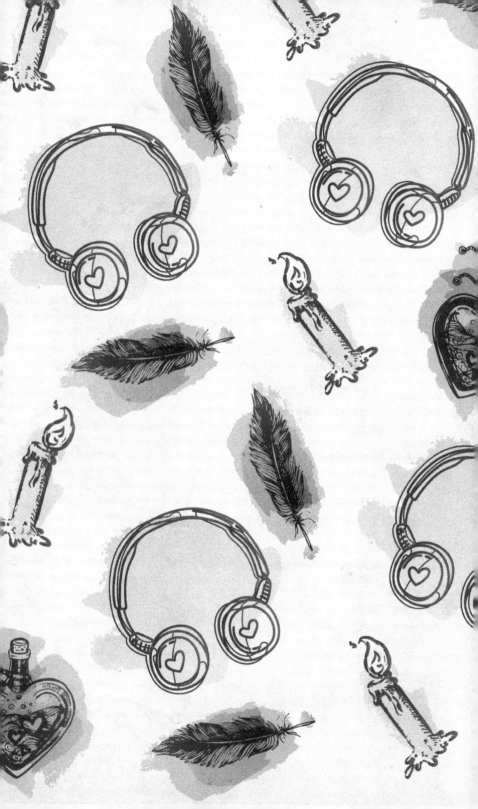

This list contains absolutely everything I will need, though I rarely use it all. As an eclectic witch, I change my mind about what I want to use during ritual all the time. There have been very glamourous rituals where I have used everything but the kitchen basin, and there have been rituals so simple and humble that I felt silly for ever purchasing all the bells and whistles. The truth is that it continues to vary even now, but the one thing that remains the same is that I always set up my altar before I cast the circle. Then I begin.

Please note, these are my words of power and the way I have chosen to perform ritual. Yours do not have to be the same. Even now, I change it up sometimes depending on my mood and purpose.

I draw a circle of salt on the floor with myself, my altar and tools inside of it. I take my wand and walk around the circle visualizing myself drawing a circle in the air around me, a sphere that contains me completely, above and below. I take my besom (broom) and walk the entire circle three times Deosil (clockwise) saying:

Element of Air, I ask you to be present and watch over my Circle.

I now walk around the circle three times holding my working candle saying:

Element of Fire, I ask you to be present and watch over my Circle.

I then walk around the circle three times sprinkling the moon water (rainwater collected on the night of the full moon) saying:

Element of Water, I ask you to be present and watch over my Circle.

Lastly, I walk the circle thrice and sprinkle the soil saying:

Element of Earth, I ask you to be present and watch over my Circle.

I then stand in the centre of my circle and say:

Element of Spirit I ask you to be present and watch over my Circle.

I then hold my wand to the sky and say:

The Circle is cast as we are between worlds, beyond the bounds of time, where night and day, birth and death, joy and sorrow meet and align. We are one.

I put the wand down and bring my hands to prayer position and say:

I align myself with you, (Goddess name), and ask you to be present in my Circle, to aid me in my working and fill me with your wisdom, love, and light. Fill me with your grace and power. Allow me the honour to know you once more.

I align myself with you, (God name), and ask that you be present in my Circle, to aid me in my working and fill me with your strength, power, and glory. Fill me with your logic and mindfulness. Allow me the honour to know you once more.

I will then take a moment to state my purpose. If it is a magickal working, I will say so and what it is I desire.

I then speak improvised words of power directly to the God and Goddess together as a pair.

The words are always different depending on the ritual and what the ritual is for.

Then, I will begin casting my spell or give thanks.

When I am entirely sure that I have finished my working, I ring the bell three times: once for the Goddess, once for the God, and once for myself. This can also represent mind, body, and spirit.

I then sit on my meditation cushion and visualize my desires manifesting into reality. When I am finished with my visualisation, I ring my bell once more. This is where I would ground myself if my energy levels are uncomfortably high.

I drink half of the wine, and then I walk about the circle with the glass and say:

I drink and take in of the Goddess.

I take a bite of the cake, and I take another turn of the circle and say:

I eat and take in the fruits of the God.

This is the part of the ritual where I share my gratitude, which again is always improvised conversation, and I normally end it with:

May we walk together in the light forever until the day, should it come, that it no longer meets our highest good.

I then say:

Elements of Earth, Air, Fire, Water, and Spirit, I thank you for your presence at my ritual and for entering my Circle. May we be intertwined and walk together in the light forever until the day, should it come, that it no longer meets our highest good.

To close my circle, I pick up my wand and walk Widdershins (anti-clockwise) around the Circle and say:

I close my Circle now. No other shall discover its presence, be affected by the energy that once manifested here, or come to any harm, discomfort, or uncertainty when they tread this ground.

Then I clean up.

This is a very basic outline of what a ritual is. What happens inside the Circle is so unique every time that it would impossible to write a complete guide for it. This ritual, though it seems short, can last anywhere between forty minutes to three hours. The ritual is your own. This is a guide. Trust me when I say if you make it yours, you will benefit far more.

Creating Your Altar

A Wiccan altar is a raised structure used for offerings, worship and prayer, and also for ritual and spell work. You may refer to this area as your shrine, though some do not associate with the term at all. The altar is often home to several items that symbolize important aspects of the Wiccan's spirituality. You may see a God and Goddess statue or two separate statues to represent them separately. You may see a cauldron, an athame, chalices, pentagrams, candles, incense, and more all representing different but crucial parts of the witch's path. There are many traditional myths and legends surrounding the altar: "let know one touch it besides yourself or face ye bad luck," "let only other witches touch it," "let everyone who enters your home touch it for luck," and the list goes on. You will find there are many myths and so called "rules" like this that you will hear. Following a path that stems from ancient worship means that things get a little muddled along the way, and not everyone agrees on the set way to do things. This is where multiple traditions and eclecticism come in handy: they provide the ability to do what feels right for you.

Traditionally speaking, a Wiccan will arrange their altar in a certain way. There will be a God side and a Goddess side. All phallic objects (such as a wand, athame, and pillar candle) will represent the God and be present on his side, and all womb-like objects (such as the cauldron, the mortar and pestle, and the chalice) shall represent the Goddess and be present on her side. In the centre there will be representation of all of the Elements: in the North, the Element of Earth (often represented by soil or sand); in the East, the Element of Air (often represented by incense or feathers); in the South, the Element of Fire (often represented with a candle flame); and in the West, the Element of Water (often represented with a bowl of water or salt). The witch will move clockwise, or "sunwise," when inviting the Elements (this is known as Deosil), and move counter clockwise when dismissing them (which is known as Widdershins). As you can see, there is a hefty amount of structure to the traditions of Wicca. However, not everyone follows these guides.

As an eclectic Wiccan witch, my altar often follows no rules—simply my desire in the moment. I like to adjust my altar eight times a year to salute the sun cycle shown in the sabbats. I rarely show any Element representation besides a single pentagram, and my God and Goddess sides vary so much that sometimes they intertwine completely. I haven't used an athame on my altar since the year 2008 because my cats were far to intrigued by it, and people often touch my representation (not out of disrespect, but to express their aesthetically pleasing nature). My altar is exceedingly eclectic and works perfectly well every time. Sometimes it has a more traditional twist and others it looks extremely unorthodox. A few years ago, I included a bunny-ear-type hairband from a fashion accessories shop on my Ostara altar, very untraditional and yet very effective because I followed my heart.

Altar Tools

You've heard all about the altar, but now let's focus on the tools that you may put on the altar. Each witch's altar is as unique as the witch, so the tools they choose to use or not use will be unique as well. I have included as many as I thought useful (including an altar decoration that can be used as a tool to some Wiccan witches). You need not use all or any of the tools if they do not appeal to you personally. You may find what you like at first will change over time, and that is all part of the beauty of being an eclectic Wiccan. Generally, the tools laid onto the altar are used during ritual. The witch will only purchase or collect what it is that they intend to actually use, although some use tools simply as decoration and that is accepted as well.

ATHAME - The ritual knife, or athame, is one of the prime Wiccan altar tools. It is traditionally a black-handled knife that represents a dagger, although in eclectic Wicca many colours and shapes are used. The athame traditionally lives in the East: the direction that represents mind, thought, and choice. However, like with all things, this is your choice. Not all athames are metal. Some are made of wood with beautiful carvings. These are often considered the less dangerous option, especially if you have children or animals within your home. The knife does not need to be sharp, as it isn't traditionally used as a knife but rather as a symbol which holds the yang energies known as the energies of the God. (You will find many phallic shaped tools are associated with the God.) The athame is used to direct energy, typically whilst casting a circle, and can also be used to cut energetic ties.

BELLS - Bells are like the Voice of the Goddess. When you ring one, it brings the Divine's attention to you and your attention to the Divine. A bell is generally selected by the witch based on the tone that he or she feels they connect with the most. A lovely tone will call beautiful, healing energy to you. Bells can also be used to clear energy. The end of a ritual is a good time for this, but if unwanted energy crops up during a ritual, then you can use the bell to disperse it.

BESOM - A broom is not necessarily classified as an altar tool, but it is indispensable for energetically cleansing sacred space.

CAULDRON - Traditionally cast-iron, a cauldron is like a 3-legged round cooking pot. You can get them in sizes from huge to tiny. Many people love the large, old-fashioned style. Today, it is much more convenient and less expensive to purchase a small one. And, realistically, they all work the same whatever the size. Put an incense charcoal in the bottom and sprinkle the herbs and powders onto it for very pagan incense.

CANDLES - Candles tend to be used to represent the different directions of North, South, East, and West. They can also be used as God and Goddess representation or Element representation. If used for the directions—also known as the corners— traditionally, one would go in each appropriate direction. For North: black, green, or brown. For East: yellow or white. For South: red

or orange. For West: blue or aqua. For Centre, where you aren't using God and Goddess candles: white, silver, or gold. Many followers of specific traditions will follow certain colours, but you do have a choice. I often change up the colours I choose to use.

CHALICE - The chalice signifies the Mother Goddess. As such, it is a yin energy altar tool. Many purchase extremely glamourous, old-style chalices to represent the Goddess. However, that is not as important as the personal representation present. A cup or wineglass of any material, even a bowl will do. Something that holds water and, ideally, is round or curvy is good. Traditionally, the altar chalice is placed in the West: the direction of Water. The Wiccan chalice is used for ceremonial drink and offering libations to the Divine.

DEITY STATUES OR IMAGES - Images or representations of any gods and goddesses who are special to you are always welcome on an altar. They are reminders of Divinity. Statues of the gods and goddesses can actually hold the vibrations of the Divine. Your altar can be your shrine or living temple where the divinity in your life dwells and stems from.

LIBATION BOWL - A small dish, bowl, or cup can go in the centre, ready to receive offerings for the gods and goddesses. However, you can also use your altar, chalice, or cauldron for this purpose.

OFFERINGS - When you honour the Divine with a gift of thanks or prayer, you can bring them to the Altar as an offering. Often, flowers or seeds are kept on the altar as an offering. You will be giving them back to Gaia, Mother Earth, later, so all offerings must be biodegradable and preferably useful to the world.

PENTACLE - a five-point star within a circle, usually placed in the centre of the altar. The pentacle offers protection and power in magickal work and can also be used to represent the Elements and the Witch's Pyramid.

SCENT OR FEATHER - Some representation of Air—commonly something scented like incense, essential oils, or smudges, or else a flying bird's feather—goes in the East.

STONES OR CRYSTALS - For the Earth Element, in the North, stones and sometimes crystals are used. You needn't spend lots of money on crystals to represent the Earth element. You have lots of other options at your disposal. Pebbles, seeds, or a little plant are effective representation.

WAND - Traditionally, the wand is made of wood (although this need not always be the case). Since all woods have unique powers, you may like to choose the wood to suit your particular needs. Or you may like to go with the wood from your birth tree. We each have a birth tree—the tree in Celtic tree lore associated with the month we were born.

Cleansing, Consecrating, and Charging

Witches make a practice of cleansing, consecrating, and charging their working tools. This act is often called the three Cs. Even though there is enough information for each of these acts to have their own section, I decided to put them together because they are often performed together. Tools are cleansed before use. This achieves a couple of things: firstly, it purifies the item before it is used to interact with the Divine. Secondly, it removes any negative energies from the tool. This is particularly handy if you aren't sure of a tool's past history or owner before it came to you. A purified object is often considered more powerful than an object that has not been cleansed. An unclean tool can be seen as a contaminated one, and a common view is its magick is likely to go awry.

Cleansing an item is much the same as washing a plate after it has been used. When you wash the plate, you remove the build-up and scrub until the plate is clean so that it can be used again and none of the remnants of the last meal are present. When we cleanse tools, we remove the remnants of energy within the tool. Some will only do this once when they first purchase, find, or are gifted the tool to remove any energies it has either been infused with or collected over time. Others may do this regularly to remove even their own energies from a tool to ensure that it has a clean slate each time they use it. To cleanse an object is just as the word implies: you are cleaning it. The difference is that you're not cleaning it on a physical level, although that can be done; what you're attempting to do is "clean" it on a spiritual level.

There are many ways of cleansing a tool. I have listed a few that I personally find to be effective.

- By use of rain or storm water (Element of Water)
- By use of "cleansing" or "purifying" incenses (Element of Air)
- Passing through a flame (Element of Fire)
- Placing the object on the Pentacle or burying it in the soil (Element of Earth)
- Asking the Element of Spirit to cleanse the object
- Placing the object in the light of the sun/moon to be cleansed by its rays/beams

Another popular act for your tools is consecration. The dictionary defines consecration as "dedication to the service and worship of a deity." Consecrating is the act of making it known to the Divine Goddess and God that these ritual tools will be used in acts of Their worship, ritual, spell, or other magickal working. To consecrate an object is to make it sacred through some minor rite or act of blessing. You can consecrate anything you want: all your tools, your jewellery, even the ground on which you hold your rituals. But do remember this: once consecrated, the item is sacred and should be treated as such.

You can consecrate an item by performing a small ritual at your altar. Traditionally, you'd need a white candle, a cup of water, a small bowl of salt, and incense. But you can vary these to suit your practice and beliefs as long as each corresponds to one of the cardinal Elements and directions:

- North/Earth: salt
- East/Air: incense
- South/Fire: candle
- West/Water: water

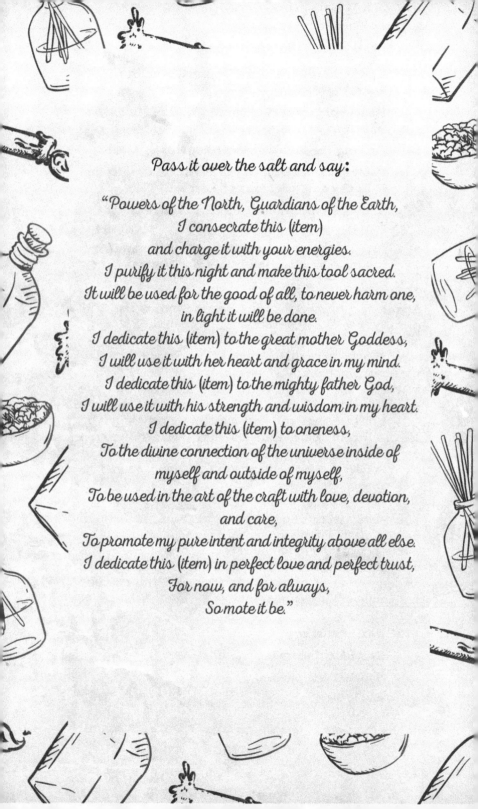

Pass it over the salt and say:

"Powers of the North, Guardians of the Earth,
I consecrate this (item)
and charge it with your energies.
I purify it this night and make this tool sacred.
It will be used for the good of all, to never harm one,
in light it will be done.
I dedicate this (item) to the great mother Goddess,
I will use it with her heart and grace in my mind.
I dedicate this (item) to the mighty father God,
I will use it with his strength and wisdom in my heart.
I dedicate this (item) to oneness,
To the divine connection of the universe inside of
myself and outside of myself,
To be used in the art of the craft with love, devotion,
and care,
To promote my pure intent and integrity above all else.
I dedicate this (item) in perfect love and perfect trust,
For now, and for always,
So mote it be."

You will then repeat the process only changing the Element and direction.

Other ways include: say a prayer over it and dedicate the use of the tool to your God and Goddess, or anoint it with blessing symbols and oils (if you keep oils that are cleansed, charged, and consecrated). Remember, you get to custom-design your practice to suit your likes, your opinions, and your associations. All colours, directions, words of power, and so on are to be those that appeal to you. Otherwise, your consecration ritual will simply be reading words from a book and copying what others have found works for them.

Charging is the last of the three Cs. Charging something empowers it with energy. You might infuse it with positive energy or charge it so its energies are aligned with some specific purpose. When we charge, we have to raise that power to put it into an object. It's much like filling your car with fuel. A car is great, but an empty one won't get you very far. There a few ways to charge an object. The simplest is to leave the object out underneath the full moon or beneath the sun. Make sure your objects are in a safe place and covered in case it should rain. Also, be sure to check that they will not be affected by potential weather damage such as extreme heat, cold, frost, water, etc. You may wish to wait until certain times of year when the weather is more predictable. If you have a greenhouse, you can simply rest them inside and the energies will penetrate through the glass windows.

You can also dance, chant, meditate, and play music to raise power. Then, pour that energy in by holding the item yourself and visualizing it becoming full. You can place the item on a previously charged crystal for a day or two so it will absorb energy, or you can use the energy you have accumulated in your other tools by either placing the item on top of them or simply keeping them all together.

Spirit Guides

A spirit guide is an incorporeal being that is gaining its personal expansion from its intent: the wish to aid, guide, assist, and also learn from another being's existence. Much like the relationship with the universal divinity of the God and Goddess, the relationship with a spirit guide is also a two-way street. The relationship is one that requires presence, awareness, acknowledgment, giving, and receiving.

Spirit guides exist in an observant form, so they will have a different perspective on your physical reality than you do because they observe without being directly emotionally or physically involved. It is commonly thought that spirit guides are a higher level of being that radiates perfection, and you must work hard to attain the same level of greatness by learning from the lessons and perspectives they share with you. This isn't true. The spirit guides are not in a physical body, but they are also going through the process of expansion as we are and so they must learn from us, too.

Some guides are with you for your entire life, whereas others may enter briefly and then leave when they have served their purpose. You can have multiple guides at one time, though this is not always the case. The spirit guide must match your energetic, vibrational frequency. So if your frequency is drastically changed either consciously or unconsciously, one of two things can happen: either the guide will leave and move to somewhere that is more of a match, or, if your personal vibrational frequency evolves over time, they will more than likely evolve with you and stay present.

A spirit guide can be a being just like you and I who has chosen not to come into the physical realm and is experiencing their current existence on a different

The spirit guide must match your energetic, vibrational frequency.

dimension. Spirit guides will align themselves with you based on the path you have taken in your physical life. For example, you may be born into a family of great wealth, and with that wealth comes opportunities and experiences that you may not otherwise experience. A spirit guide that has been searching for someone living that life and experiencing that physical enactment here in the third dimension may decide to attach to you in order to learn from your physical experiences and to promote their own spiritual expansion in a non-physical realm. As a result of your relationship and connection, they will help you stay on course and move toward your highest good. They often have a better perspective on the bigger picture than you do based on their perception standpoint.

Sometimes your spirit guide will be a relation who has passed on and is now guiding you through this life. This does not make them a ghost. They are not manifested into a physical body in this life because they choose not to be. It just means that this family member has been reborn into a reality where they have chosen to either remember their previous life entirely or stay connected to it consciously for the purpose of personal growth. It may be they desire to experience the process of grief that you go through after they have passed. Sometimes, a family-connected guide can need to experience life as the opposite gender or in an opposite role: a father who passes may wish to see life from his daughter's perspective in order to gain insight on his spiritual journey, or a daughter who may wish to learn from her mother or brother. Whatever the reason, the choice to work with you needs to be valuable for them in terms of expansion. It is not uncommon for a spirit guide to be a family member, although this may never be the case for some of us. It may be that if a sibling or close family member passes that they may not need to revisit this life and learn from your experience because they have already experienced something very similar themselves. If a friend's guide is a family member and your guides are not, do not feel sad or resentful. It is simply that your friend's family guide had something valuable to learn by accessing her current channel to the physical realm and your relative did not.

Sometimes a spirit guide will not be a manifestation of a human at all, but rather an animal guide. This is what some Native American tribes commonly refer to as animal totems. In truth, it is possible that your guide could be anything or anyone that matches your vibrational frequency and that feels they can assist you and equally learn from you.

Another type of spirit guide—and most common within your life—is your higher self. This guide is the expression of the manifestation of yourself that exists in the non-physical dimensions.

The Witch's Familiar

A witch's familiar is a spiritual entity that embodies an animal within the third dimension or physical realm. The spirit of the familiar can be ongoing even when the physical body of the animal passes away. You may go through your entire spiritual journey only ever connecting to one specific spiritual entity. However, it may manifest itself time and time again in different animals. Sometimes these animals will be pets and other times they will be wild animals that visit you. You may even find that a pet of a neighbour turns out to be your familiar. You may have many different familiar spiritual entities throughout your practice, and there is a chance they will overlap.

I have had two different spiritual entity energies appear as familiars throughout my practice so far. One was only a very brief encounter that lasted about six weeks: a pure white, long-haired cat that came to my garden every night and sat in exactly the same spot. I never saw the cat before and have never seen it since. I assumed it was owned by someone visiting a neighbour. On that particular occasion, the spirit of the familiar was entirely new to me. It had a message that I would soon come to realise would aid me greatly in my spiritual path and personal growth. The last time I saw the white cat was the day I realised what the message was. The other familiar spirit energy has manifested in my life in three different forms. Two of those forms were animals that both happened to be pets. The first, strangely enough, was a ginormous koi carp that was the proudest possession of my father.

We had a large pond in the back garden, and despite it

being hard to interact with a fish, Oscar the koi did a wonderful job. He would suckle my finger daily and—on occasion—jump out of the pond entirely. It was when I was sitting on the pond wall and contemplating existence and the big questions that I first discovered Wicca and my belief system. Many years later, that familiar returned to me in the form of a pet cat named Luna. She still graces me with her presence today. She loves my Book of Shadows and is always present for updates. She can't get enough of my crystals, and my altar is the best seat in the house. I have another cat named Nala. Lovable as she is, she is definitely not a familiar to me. Who knows what she gets up to all day long?

The animal will work with the witch in order to aid his or her magickal working and help guide them along their spiritual path. In traditional Wicca, it is often viewed that the familiar will pick the witch and not the other way around (although opinions vary throughout belief systems). The familiar can perform non-physical tasks for the witch in order to help him or her. If a witch is doing astral projection work, then they can ask their familiar to come with them on their journey and help guide them home to their physical bodies. Sometimes an act may be physical. However, this tends to be when the familiar performs an action from their own agenda in order to help guide the witch.

When writing this book, I spent several hours each day working on the content. Luna spent the entire day inside with me each time. Usually, she would be outdoors soaking up the sun and playing with her feline sister. But when I was writing she was constantly present, so much so that one night, after thirteen hours of straight writing, she came and lay on my keyboard to tell me it was time for bed. And she was right. By that point, I had lost all sense of direction. I ended up deleting the last four pages I had written the next day after I read them back.

Some witches believe that a familiar does not necessarily manifest in the form of an animal. Some believe plants and trees to be their familiars, and others are certain that their familiar spirit exists inside an inanimate object. This is a less popular belief, though it is a belief all the same.

There may be periods of time, long or short, when you either do not feel the presence of a familiar at all or feel the presence of one but are not aware of where it is. Before Luna came into my life, there was a period of about three years when I still felt the presence of my familiar spirit. To this day, I have no idea where it was residing. I thought at one point it was inside of a necklace that I wore daily, but I am honestly not sure.

The Book of Shadows

A Book of Shadows is often considered a witch's most personal and prized possession. In traditional Wicca, a Book of Shadows is a book containing religious texts and instructions for magickal rituals found within Wicca. Each witch possesses their own. The Book was said to be a plain black leather book, although today witches have books of all colours, shapes, and sizes, made up of many different materials. Many Wiccans use a three-ring binder as their first Book of Shadows because it allows them to reorganise the pages when they wish to. Only much later will they transfer the information into a book. It was also said that the Book must be written by hand, but today many witches choose to use a computer to print out the text. Some witches even keep their Book of Shadows on their computer entirely, although it is a good idea to back it up to an external hard drive. Technology can still fail.

Eclectic Wiccans use the Book much like a journal. They may still include religious texts and magickal rituals, but they also write their innermost thoughts, feelings, and desires. The Book can be used as a way of documenting and recording your ritual and spell work, and can also be used to make entries of your spiritual journey. Today, a Book of Shadows can contain a great many things and I shall list some of them below.

- **A Book Blessing**
- **History of Wicca**
- **Religious text such as the Wiccan Rede**
- **Rituals**
- **Spell work**
- **Photographs or drawings of altar setups**
- **Photographs of yourself, family, or loved ones**
- **Diary entries**
- **Information on the sabbats and ideas on how to celebrate**
- **Documents of how you celebrate**
- **Information on the Lunar cycle**
- **Esbat information**
- **Divination tools**

- Familiars
- Meditation
- Grounding
- Visualisation
- Words of power
- The Theban alphabet
- God and Goddess information
- Different pantheons you are interested in
- Lists of herbs and their properties
- Lists of crystals and their properties
- Lists of incenses and their properties
- Lists of essential oils and their properties
- Ritual bathing
- Sacred site information and photographs
- Animal guides and spirit animals
- Spirit guides
- Information on the Elements
- The Four Powers of Magus or the Witch's Pyramid
- Thirteen principles of belief
- The Threefold Law
- Information on chakras
- Information on auras
- Information on colour therapy
- Information on candle magick
- Information on handmade crafts
- Pagan chants and songs
- The Charge of the Goddess
- Drawing down the moon
- The Charge of the Crone

- 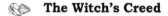 **The Witch's Creed**
- **The Charge of the God**
- **The Great Rite Invocation**
- **Profiles on historically famous Wiccans**
- **Self-love**
- **Shadow work**

The list could literally go on and on forever. Because humans are ever-evolving beings, we tend to fill many Books of Shadows over the span of one lifetime. It is quite common to have already found or purchased a new one before the old one is even full. This is the witch's own personal sanctuary where he or she can be entirely themselves. Many witches choose to keep their Book of Shadows entirely private and not show its contents to even their nearest and dearest. However, there are those who do not mind sharing some content publicly. I have shared parts of my Book of Shadows publicly on my website and with clients, friends, and family, but there are still elements I keep private and for my eyes only.

The Broom Closet

The Broom Closet is a term Wiccans use to describe whether their path, belief, or religion are public to those around them or something they keep to themselves. Upon taking the first steps on their spiritual journey, many Wiccans keep their knowledge and experiences private.

Secrecy is not a requirement of Wicca, quite the opposite in fact. Most who are still in the broom closet are attempting to find the right time and way to open the door and show people what hangs inside. When Wiccans do choose to stay private it can be for many reasons. New Wiccans, when they are discovering an entirely new belief system, often feel more comfortable keeping it private until they are sure the path suits them fully. This is somewhere they intend to stay for the foreseeable future. Some Wiccans feel forced to keep their beliefs a secret. They may find themselves being raised in a home of another religion and do not wish to cause offence to strictly religious parents. They may find themselves living in an area that has very little understanding of Wicca and no desire to gain any knowledge. As a result, the Wiccan can feel as though they would be isolated for speaking of their beliefs publicly.

Some people are what is referred to as "partially out of the broom closet." Sometimes this is called having a foot out of the door or simply keeping the door to the closet ajar. Some Wiccans are happy to share their faith with their friends and partners but not with family members of older generations or potentially their work colleagues.

Some Wiccans, like myself, were never really in the broom closet to begin with. Though I was raised in a Christian household, my parents were always extremely open to me and my sister expressing ourselves in our

own way and learning about life in the way we saw fit. As long as we weren't in danger or in trouble, they were supportive. I was extremely lucky. I discovered Wicca back in 1998, and at the time we didn't have the sources available to us that we do today. To learn about Wicca meant going to the library to take out a book or two from an extremely small collection that often covered witchcraft as a whole topic rather than Wicca as a subject. Many of the books back then focussed on the burning times and the history of witchcraft rather than modern-day Wicca. My parents helped me discover the information I desired to research and were happy to support my choices. In 2005, my father took my family and I on a trip to Glastonbury, England, and there he purchased my very first cauldron as a gift.

To say I was surprised would be an understatement. It was a medium-sized black cauldron that stood about eight inches tall. I remember when I first got my cat she fit inside it completely and often slept there.

I do not remember a time that I stood before my parents and said "Mum, Dad...I am a witch!" If it did happen, then it obviously wasn't memorable. It was simply accepted that I was just a bit different. Not odd, not wrong, not weird and kooky, just different. Unlike my mum, who would say her prayers to the Christian God at nighttime before bed, I would cast mine in the form of a spell within ritual. The only conflict that ever arose during my practice was when I was a teenager. I would often remove the batteries from my fire alarm to stop it from howling like a banshee when I lit dozens of candles, and my parents did not like that.

The broom closet is a little wall that is put in place for your own comfort. Some Wiccans love the freedom of secrecy and having the wall in place. They do not hide behind it, but rather lean up against it and are shielded from the opinions of the world. Some Wiccans find the wall to be a lonely and suppressive place to sit behind. They wish they could gather their strength to knock it down, and one day they will. Everyone comes out in their own time and stays in for their own purpose. It is not better or worse to be in or out of the broom closet. It doesn't change the fact that you believe what you believe.

The Natural World

THE SPIRIT

Part Three

The Spiritual Journey

I am sure by now you can see that embracing the path of an eclectic Wiccan is no walk in the park. The work load is endless, the studies continuous, the growth enormous, and the analysing enough to make your brain frazzle. But I can honestly say without a shadow of a doubt it is so worth it. Every single step I have taken on the yellow brick road of witchery has taken me closer and closer to becoming exactly who I wanted to be: living my dreams and manifesting my desires into reality before my very eyes. Have I made mistakes along the way? Too many to count. Have I failed miserably at conducting rituals and spell work? I still do at times, and I'm eighteen years into my journey. There is not one thing I would go back and change about taking that leap into the world of Wicca back in 1998. Every trial, tribulation, and obstacle I have faced has taught me a well-needed lesson. Every goal I have achieved has placed another brick on the sturdy wall that is my confidence in my own abilities. If you have come this far and you are still on the fence, then I urge you to stay there for a while. It's never a good idea to jump into murky waters. But if you can see now more clearly than you ever have before, then dive head first in to the crystal lake of magick and be cleansed of all that came before. Cleanse, but never forget.

Connecting to the God
and Goddess

One of the most beautiful things about the connection to the divine is that you need not be anything other than what you already are to feel the presence, celebrate the greatness, and acknowledge the power of divinity inside and outside of yourself. Many people find themselves struggling to find the divine feminine or divine masculine within. This is generally because they find themselves hunting for a part of them that is unattainable and unrealistic.

All living beings have aspects of both divine feminine and divine masculine within them. We are made up of both, though at certain times we may feel more connected to one than the other. Just because you are born into this life as a female being does not necessarily mean you will automatically feel more connected to the Goddess or divine feminine, and the same goes for those who were born into this life as a male. They too will not necessarily feel most connected to the divine masculine or God.

For many thousands of years there has been a disconnect from the divine feminine based on the society and how it has viewed women as a whole. Power roles of women have definitely shifted in more recent years. However, that does not change the core belief that many of us still carry deeply inside: the suspicion that being female or connecting with the feminine makes us somehow second class. I was taught by my authority figures that being born a female had set me up in life with certain disadvantages. There were certain clothes I was expected to wear and certain clothes I was not. There were appropriate haircuts, ways in which to behave, language that I was allowed to use, and directions in which it would be most proper for me to take my life.

As the potential bearer of children, I was told it was almost certain that I would reach a certain age and reproduce offspring. I would most likely marry a man and take his surname as my own. I would leave my previous self behind and settle into my new roles as a wife and mother. The women who didn't do these things were odd, selfish, living unfulfilled lives of fantasy, or had their sexuality questioned. Being raised in a society that tells a girl she cannot run as fast, she isn't as strong, she is too emotional, she is not as rational as a boy is severely damaging. That damage interferes with a connection to the divine feminine. And a little girl can begin to hear these poisonous outside statements approximately around the age of three years old.

Each woman is a unique expression of the Goddess. The divine feminine manifests in each man as well, also as a unique expression of the Goddess. When the feminine aspects of self are restricted, we are limiting a connection with the Goddess. We are being untrue to ourselves and to the very nature of what makes up the feminine divinity within us. A connection with the Goddess does not stem from that which houses us in a neat little box or category. Instead, it grows from the place that allows us as individuals to be our own unique expression of what it is to be feminine in our perception of reality.

The divine energy is made up of oneness. The universe as a whole is life source energy. One great force of continuous existence, and one of the manifestations within the universe, is polarity: contrasting opposites. The contrasting opposites of the universe are that of feminine and masculine energy, the feminine being the Goddess and the masculine being the God. The duality of the universe is sacred because it represents two categories of aspects within the universe that we see, feel, and experience every day of our lives.

As a direct result of being raised in a society that had chosen my role for me long before my parents had even considered having children, I grew up to have a long list of insecurities surrounding my lack of feminine traits. I struggled to walk in heels, I had little to no interest in gossip and chatter, and I was not part of some large herd of other females.

Much later in life, I realised that femininity is not and never was about society's standards for women, certainly not in the eyes of the Goddess. When we look back throughout history, the Goddesses that fill our text books were not worshipped, valued, or respected for their ability to parade around in high heels like elegant gazelles, to be seen but not heard by their male counterparts, or to exist entirely to bear the fruit of their lovers. This does not mean they did not possess great beauty, but, like everything, beauty comes in all shapes and sizes.

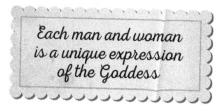

Each man and woman
is a unique expression
of the Goddess

The Goddesses, or aspects of the divine feminine, were worshipped because of their capabilities, their resourcefulness, and their comprehension of what it is to be a balanced human being. Their strength and intelligence is what gave them their beauty, and their dexterity and might gave them their love. The divine feminine of the Goddess—and of each of us—does not exist in society's version of what little girls should grow up to be.

The divine feminine encompasses all that we are: the vulnerable and the strong, the life-giver and the wielder of protection to her children. The divine feminine is a mother and a warrior in the same breath. She would bear her child and take the life of another if she saw fit to do so. She is not stone. She is water; she is fluid. Her emotions run deep like a bottomless river of solitude, despair, and dismay, but here she swims to find her spirit: the valiant gentility that only comes with understanding who you are entirely. The Goddess is not free from fear or worry. She is not free from heartache and pain. She is nothing and everything at once.

The divine feminine calls for nothing inside you to be present that is not already present. No clothing or hairstyle can aid your connection with her spirit. No soft-spoken girlish manner or fair appearance will catch her eye. The Goddess does not see the shell you wear in this lifetime. She sees the makeup of your soul. She connects to your strength, your integrity, and your will.

Every aspect that ever existed inside of you or any other living creature also exists inside the Goddess. So there is no manner in which you must behave to represent the Goddess and connect with her, for she is ever-present in every aspect of you that is intertwined with her endless love for the God.

The feminine aspects of the universe are:

WISDOM – the quality of having experience, knowledge, and good judgement; the quality of being wise.
FORGIVENESS – the action or process of forgiving or being forgiven.
CONNECTION – a relationship in which a person or thing is linked or associated with something else.
RESTORATION – restoring all life to its highest condition.
UNDERSTANDING – having insight or good judgement.
COMPASSION – sympathetic pity and concern for the sufferings or misfortunes of others.
SENSUALITY – the enjoyment, expression, or pursuit of pleasure.
RENEWAL – the instance of resuming to a former state.
CREATION – the action or process of bringing something into existence.
HEALING – the process of making or becoming sound or healthy again.
OPENESS – unrestricted access to that which comes.
LIFE – the capacity for growth, reproduction, functional activity, and continual change preceding death.
BIRTH – the emergence of a new creation from the body of its mother or former shell; the start of life as a physically separate being.

RECEPTIVITY – ability to receive.
NURTURING – to help or encourage development.
LOVE – a strong feeling of intense connection,
emotion, and affection.

I feel it is important for me to express that though the
divine feminine inside of us is not connected to the
way we dress or choose to present ourselves to society
on the surface, there is certainly no lack of Goddess
connection in those who choose to wear dresses and
heels. It is simply irrelevant that some may choose to
do so. The divine feminine is just as present within
men as it is within women. It may be seen differently
on the surface and even experienced differently in the
traits they possess.

From a young age, a boy's mind is penetrated with the
knowledge of what it is to be male in the same way that
a young girl is told what it is to be female. The boy is
faster, stronger, and more logical. When he cries, he is
shamed for showing his feminine side in the eyes of the
society. When he takes great care in his appearance,
he is tormented and labelled weak. He is to take what
he wants and work endlessly. As a direct result, many
young men grow up to be emotionally unavailable later
in life.

The truth is: no matter how often he cries or how long
he takes to do his hair and choose his clothes, he is
no less masculine than any other man. Nor is he more
feminine than any other man. The balance of divinity is
equal inside all of us, though some do not acknowledge
what comes naturally. This does not mean that all
men will express themselves the same way. Some men
choose to wear high heels because they love the way
they look and feel, but these men do not necessarily
present any other stereotypical female qualities.

The man who society deems to be strong, fast, and
stoney may be very emotional and soft inside, but

presents neither female nor male divinity at a higher or lower presence.

The God is as ever-present inside every woman. Just like the connection with the Goddess, there is no way to have any more or any less of a connection with the God within yourself. It is always present in the way it is meant to be. Each living creature on the planet is a direct expression of the God and Goddess, just as each God and Goddess is a direct expression of some aspect of the universe.

The way you express yourself is simply one way the female and male divine has chosen to be present within you. Society may have very clear-cut standards of what it is to be a man and what it is to be a woman, but they are child's play in the vast spectrum of creation that allows the embodiment of divinity to present inside each individual being.

To fully connect to the sacred divinity, we must release the resistance to our gender. Men are often labelled as having a deep competitive hierarchy within their cores. However, this is only one aspect of the sacred divine masculine. It may not display presence in all who connect with the God. There is a common misconception that the sacred masculine energy supports that of a power struggle, where men (or even one man) must be above or on top of a pyramid and all others must obey and be below him. This field of thinking has given us Abrahamic religions, war, and slavery, not to mention a number of other unpleasant circumstances and situations. Domination and control is not of the divine masculine. It is a shadow aspect that societies take on to define what it means to be a certain gender.

The masculine aspects of the universe are:

MOVEMENT – working together to advance shared political, social, or artistic ideas.

ACTION – the act or process of achieving an aim.

RESPONSIBILITY – the state of being accountable.

INTELLECT – the faculty of reasoning and understanding objectively, especially with regard to abstract matters.

STRENGTH – the quality or state of being mentally or physically capable.

MATERIAL ABUNDANCE – a copious supply; great amount of material substance in mind, body, and spirit.

DIRECTION – the management or guidance of someone or something.

CLARITY – the quality of being coherent and intelligible.

FOCUS – to pay particular attention to what is needed.

GENOROSITY – the quality of being kind and generous.

ENCOURAGMENT – the action of giving someone support, confidence, or hope.

TRANSFORMATION – a marked change in form, nature, or appearance.

GROWTH – the process of increasing.

Each man and woman is a unique expression of divine masculine

Each man and woman is a unique expression of divine masculine. Each man and woman is a unique expression of divine feminine. Connection with your inner sacred divine is not an act of deciding what masculinity or femininity is or isn't and then conforming to that idea. It is about finding out what unique expression of the sacred divine is taking place inside you. Creating divine connection is the action of you discovering how to come into alignment with the God and Goddess, and that will be very different from the way the person next to you does it.

Drawing Down the Moon

If you have ever read any books on Wicca before, you may have come across the phrase "drawing down the moon." It sounds very elegant and artistic, but what does it mean? Drawing down the moon is a trance technique explained differently by every witch. Basically, it is a form of opening yourself like a vessel or flower to the wisdom of the Goddess. You still have the presence of your conscious mind and body, but they are almost like observers as opposed to participants. The energies and information come from deep within yourself and also from outside of yourself. They penetrate your psyche, creating an experience like that of being in a metaphorical womb. This ritual is most commonly done on the full moon. However, if you are wishing to connect with the Maiden aspect of the Goddess, you may choose to perform at the waxing moon, or the waning moon for the Crone aspect. It is a way to fully experience the divine feminine within yourself.

Some traditions believe that this act should only ever be performed by women, although that is not the belief for all. It is a very beautiful technique, and it gifts us with the memory that the sacred divine feminine exists deep inside each of us.

Drawing Down the Sun

This is a technique that is commonly thought to be used by men, although, just as with drawing down the moon, the opposite gender can use either of these techniques as ritual. It is the means in which the God is invoked and drawn into the witch and communed with, similarly to the above ritual technique with the Goddess, and the moon. Attaining solar illumination is the goal here, so as to feel and connect to the God within you. The consciousness is heightened, and often you will receive the ability to see what is ordinarily unseen by the human eye. This is a way of directly communicating with the divine masculine: to see and be seen.

Both of these techniques are similar in conducting performance, but with very different results.

With drawing down the moon, we are experiencing the Goddess in whichever cycle we choose and depending on which moon phase we choose to work the magick. It could be a young Maiden Goddess, a full-bellied Mother Goddess, or a wise old Crone Goddess. With drawing down the sun, we are going to experience the different Lunar Gods in whichever form is in alignment with the season and time of year. The results will vary greatly in springtime to winter and in summertime to autumn. On the other hand, the moon cycle is so much shorter in length than the changing of seasons throughout the year, so the varying degrees are considered more frequent. Often, because of this, many witches will claim to have more of a connection with a specific Goddess rather than with the Gods, although the connection to the divine masculine in general can still be as strong.

Drawing down the moon and the sun are techniques for an altered state of consciousness, a ritual possession by the Divine. It is not uncommon to feel the energy of the Goddess and/or God for quite some time following the ritual, so don't be alarmed if you feel a heightened sense of clarity over the next few days. You may also feel extremely emotional; it is uncommon to carry out the ritual without a few tears or even laughter.

There are many versions and ways to perform these sacred divine rituals used to draw power into yourself and, if you wish, to channel wisdom from a higher source. You can use them either for a specific purpose or for increasing your spiritual awareness, which is very common.

This ritual can be carried out alone or with a group. Traditionally, in a coven setting, it is the High Priestess who draws down the moon and the High Priest who draws down the sun into themselves and then channels the wisdom so that each coven member can absorb the power in his or her own way and experience the connection between the individual divine spark and the collective Divinity.

Intuition

We are all blessed with a divine internal guidance system known as our intuition. It is the voice that alerts us to the path, people, and circumstances that we will uniquely find fulfilling, and it keeps us away from danger and harm. Albert Einstein once said that it is our most valuable asset and one of our most unused sense. The intuition is not just an odd feeling in your gut that gives you butterflies every once in a while. It is a crucial tool needed to function fully, just like any other sense you have. You would not cross the road without first checking to see if you could see or hear anything coming. You physically cannot cross the road without your sense of touch, and with your senses of smell and taste go hand-in-hand with alerting you to safety or danger. Crossing a road without using your intuition is dangerous, and existing your entire life without hearing it could be fatal.

Many of us stop communicating with our intuition, the internal voice of the soul, at a young age. The inner voice rarely speaks to us in a language. Although it can happen, it more often than not speaks to us in sensations—acting out by creating a feeling of unease when we consider doing something it doesn't like, or creating a feeling of warmth and honour when we act in our highest favour.

Our society is a busy one with authority figures left and right. We live on rules, regulations, and time schedules. Our soul wasn't designed for them. It is not uncommon to go to work five days a week, or even six, to the same building. We go week-in and week-out, year-in and year-out, to do the same task every single day. Our soul wants us to grow, expand, and evolve. It wants us to live and to learn from our experiences and joys. Society tells us we cannot be happy all the time, that happiness must be earned and must come in second to all of the responsibilities we have to undertake simply to exist on the planet today. The soul was designed many years before currency existed, let alone ran our whole world. The soul doesn't exist in deadlines, rules, or regulations. It always evolves in new and progressive ways that cannot be recorded by time or altered in any way. Even if we could record

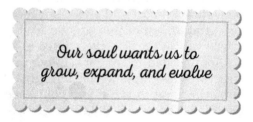

Our soul wants us to grow, expand, and evolve

the progress of the soul, every single soul would be a unique expression of Existence itself, so we would only ever be able to judge that one soul at any one time.

Intuition is a direct link to the soul, like receiving a phone call. The law may say this, your boss may say that, your teacher may say other, but only your soul knows what it needs to evolve. Given the choice, we continuously respond to the authorities of society because the punishment of not obeying is so much worse. The soul never punishes; it simply takes longer to move forward into an ascended state, and, in some cases, it doesn't get the chance before we pass on because we get so involved in society that we stop hearing the phone call altogether.

When we do not listen to our intuition, the only hope our soul has of getting the messages through is by being louder and more physical, so we develop physical symptoms such as migraines, stomach aches, and pains. When the intuition is ignored for a long time, the body will manifest disease as a result. This is the only way your internal self can show your external self that it is in desperate need of attention.

Many times on your spiritual journey, you will read or hear that it is wise to listen to your intuition and to ignore your ego. You will hear that the ego is made up of the lies we tell ourselves that are filtered down to us through what is external, such as society's standards of who we should be, and that our intuition

Intuition is a direct link to the soul

is the purest truth of the universe. Though one sounds much more pleasant that the other, the participation of both is crucial in your spiritual journey because both are you and always will be. The voice of ego and the voice of intuition are ever-changing, but they will always reflect you no matter how positive or negative they sound. If you try to sever the connection with your ego, then you will also sever the connection with your intuition. You need both to create a balance that aligns with your highest good. The ego is where many of our most important lessons lie.

Perspective

As universal consciousness temporarily projecting itself into our third dimensional reality, as human beings, we often perceive ourselves to be separate to the energy of other beings and objects around us. It is easy enough for us to see ourselves as different entirely from our neighbour or our ex-partner's new spouse. However, this is simply a perception, which does not make it true. We are as much at one with a human being living across the other side of the globe, despite the fact that we have never met this person, as we are with ourselves. Not only are we connected to other people, but we are also connected to every tree in every forest, every droplet of water that trickles in the springs of the highest mountains, and every blade of grass that we feel beneath our bare feet that exists or has ever existed. We are all universal consciousness temporarily being projected into our current reality.

We see the world as individual beings so that we can grow and ascend as individual beings. But at the most fundamental level, everything in existence is you, and you are everything in existence.

If we take a closer look at projection, we learn the very definition of the word is an unconscious self-defence mechanism characterised by a person unconsciously attributing their own issues or desires onto someone or something else as a form of delusion and denial. We see this often in relationships. When one person falls for another temporarily whilst in the bliss of a new relationship, person A can project their desire and infatuation onto person B, which leaves person A almost certain that person B feels exactly the same way. In reality, even if both people feel infatuation and desire for one another, the results of those feelings will manifest differently in each person due to a lifetime of differences. What person A is unaware of in this situation is that they are simply perceiving person B to feel the same way because they have projected their own feelings onto them. This is an individual approach to existence where person A and person B are separate beings.

In our multi-dimensional reality, we can perceive ourselves as individuals or we can perceive ourselves as the collective consciousness of the universe. Either way, we still are exactly what we are: energy. We can choose our perception based on how we believe it will help our spirituality expand, and we can chop and change as often as we like. In the individual perspective, person A and person B are separate projections of the universe. In the universal consciousness perspective, person A and person B are the same person. As individuals, we experience our entire reality as a reflection of the different aspects within ourselves made up of universal consciousness.

Dream Work

When we sleep, our consciousness or conscious mind returns to a non-physical perspective. When we dream, what we are experiencing is a higher-frequency dimensional reality. We achieve that state by having a form of out-of-body experience. The higher-frequency dimension that we experience as reality whilst we are sleeping is a time and space in a process of potential existence, a time and space that are yet to manifest in our conscious reality. We know we are experiencing an out-of-body experience to a certain degree. If we were not, our bodies would act out everything that we experience in our dreams and our physical bodies would be in conscious danger.

When we are sleeping, the motor function aspect of our brain is, for the most part, disabled. We can sometimes think that we are dreaming all night long, but this is not the case. Our brains perceive linear time. When we go to sleep, we withdraw our consciousness back to the source perspective or universe perspective.

A lot of what we experience in dreams—like the ability to fly, become invisible, and walk on water—are things that we would consider to be impossible in our reality in the third dimension here on Earth. But they are possible in our dreams. It's not purely because of imagination, but rather because whilst asleep our consciousness travels to a non-physical perspective of different, higher-frequency dimensions that are not as limited as the one in which we live out our conscious, awakened reality. It is very hard for our waking mind to process this information because it is used to existing in a place where such things are considered impossible. So our brain must translate this information to us almost as though it is a foreign language, and this language is communicated to us in the form of dreams.

Your dreams are always a vibrational match to what you have been thinking, feeling, and experiencing in your conscious, awake life. This is why so much of our dreams often feels extremely familiar. Dreams are a preview of a pre-manifested reality that has not yet become a physical reality in the dimension in which we currently exist.

Dreams are a fantastic tool for understanding the Law of Attraction. That which we focus on will manifest and become our reality. Have you ever had a dream where you wished really hard something wouldn't happen only to turn your head and see that very thing appearing before your eyes? This is because you were focusing so hard that you manifested it into your reality. Things may not work quite so instantaneously whilst you are awake, but they do work in the same way.

Dreams can teach us many things, including how to accept instead of resist. Many of us struggle with extreme resistance whilst awake, and, again, we focus on what it is we don't want. Then, we realise we have created an abundance of that very thing in our lives. Our dream-selves, though they may wish very strongly that something will not present itself in the dream, have a very different way of handling its presence. In real life, you may be so resistant to the idea of your business failing that you actually manifest financial issues. As a result, you become stressed, sleep-deprived, physically unwell, and riddled with anxiety. In a dream, the same person who can barely drag themselves off the couch in real life will battle a Tyrannosaurus with a saucepan and win! Because your dream-self does not focus on what they can't achieve, but rather what they can, they refuse to waste their energies on resisting the problem.

There are many things we go through in life that we are so resistant to experiencing and feeling that we attempt to sweep them under the rug because we convince ourselves that it's an easier way to cope. We will then experience an abundance of dreams about those very same situations

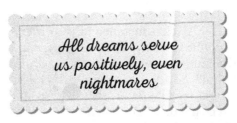

All dreams serve us positively, even nightmares

every time we go to sleep. This is because our mind needs to process this information somehow. We physically cannot function without moving through this heavy work, and when our awake-selves say no, our dream-selves say yes. The lack of resistance in dreams means that all of those suppressed and hidden emotions, situations, and circumstances can be slowly worked through whilst we are asleep. Our subconscious mind translates these video messages (of sorts) to our conscious mind so that over time, all of these issues will be resolved and dealt with properly whether we are awake or asleep.

When our dreams present us with reoccurring themes, we are handed a vibrational match to our waking lives. If you often dream of running away from something or someone, then the chances are that in your waking life you feel either uncomfortable, unsafe, or the need to escape. If your often dream of a lost lover returning to you, then the chances are that in your waking life you feel the need to reconnect with that person or still have issues surrounding the end of the relationship and are creating closure for yourself in sleep.

All dreams serve us positively, even nightmares. Those of us experiencing nightmares are experiencing states of emotional distress in our waking lives that we are either unaware of or do not know how to resolve.

Many people are confused by the idea that a Tyrannosaurus rex appearing in your dreams could be a direct link to the way you are feeling in your awakened life. The predator in your dreams is a metaphorical manifestation of how you feel under the pressure in your awakened life.

The real issue or circumstance in your everyday life may be a person who is always hounding you and bringing you an overwhelming sense of desperation to flee away from them. It could be the upcoming exams you're facing at school that you would do nearly anything to escape. Or it could even be the new baby you are expecting, and you are terrified that you won't be ready for when he or she arrives. It is rare to experience the actual person or circumstance that is bothering you in your waking life in dreams. If you ever do, they may still be displayed in a different situation. The link is how it leaves you feeling. The thing or circumstance appearing in your dreams is a symbolic representation of your waking life and the emotional ties to what is happening or what you are thinking or feeling.

So now that we understand this, what can we do about it? Well, the good news is that we can use dream work to help us not only understand our dreams, but to also help us work through the scenarios and issues that are creating them in the first place. One of the most effective ways of interpreting your dreams is to dream journal.

Dream journaling is the act of recording your dreams in a book, by audio, or by video, for yourself. Most find it effective to do this in the morning as soon as they wake up, as dreams can become foggy and difficult to remember throughout the day. Waking up and making a record of your dreams in as much detail as possible is the physical act of dream journaling. Whether you attempt to interpret the dreams then and there or whether you have to come back to them later depends on your preference, lifestyle, and schedule.

There are many useful books, websites, etc. to help you analyse and dissect your dreams, but a lot of the messages being shown to you can be quite obvious with a little thought in relation to what is currently going on in your life whilst awake.

A list of questions I find useful to ask myself when analysing my dreams are:

How did this scenario make me feel emotionally and physically?

Is there anything in my life currently that makes me feel the same way?

Have I had this dream before or a similar kind, and if so, when was this and what was going on in my life at that time?

Can I find direct links between right now in my waking life and what was happening in my life at previous times when I have had similar dreams?

What is it that specifically made me feel.................... in my dream?

What in my waking life has caused me to feel ....before?

Include any of your own questions to help analyse your dreams and make a record of your interpretations. Over time, you will find that you begin to interpret without even realising you are doing so, and you will find your dreams last longer in your mind. I have been analysing my dreams for many years, and I can honestly say I don't remember the last time I didn't remember a dream. My dreams stay with me like memories.

Finding Your Bliss

Many people of today's world feel torn, overwhelmed, and frustrated with life in general. We constantly compare ourselves to others asking questions like:

Why can't I do that?
Why don't I have those abilities?
Why don't I look that way?
Why don't I perform that way?

Each and every one of us deals with things differently. It doesn't matter what personality assessment you like –DISC, Enneagram, 5 Languages of Love, or any of the many other personality assessments. The outcome is the same: we are all different and we approach problems, situations, and problem-solving differently. We may come from the same place, we may be made up of the same things, but our expression here on the third dimension is different.

Take a look at a flower—a rose, to be more precise. Each rosebud grows from the same plant, is watered in the same soil, is a collective of expressions of the bush itself. However, no two roses are identical, and not just in appearance, but in their makeup as well. Just like each individual rose, we are also very different: part of the collective consciousness that makes up the divine universe, but uniquely designed to serve a purpose.

As children we struggle to fit in, terrified to be the outcast. As adults we fight to stand out, worried we will lose our identities in the vast blanket of statistics. Always fighting so hard, always resisting, focussing so directly on what it is we don't want that we hardly ever have the time to stop and ask ourselves what it is we do want. Priorities in our lives tend to be family, finance, housing, etc. In other words: things that move us ahead, things that keep us on the ride. What we want and who we are become of very little importance in a world where we find ourselves sending emails and making phone calls even in the restroom. Many people go in search of their spiritual awakening in hopes of finding happiness, a better life, and a more serene way of living, but the truth is that no matter what book you follow, which Gods you worship, or how many times you dance naked under the full moon, happiness isn't spirituality. Spirituality is you. It is all that you are. It is every up and every down. But that does not mean the two cannot be linked.

Finding happiness through spirituality is not about who or what you follow, but rather about following and honouring yourself, your feelings, your beliefs, and your priorities.

Think for a moment: if you were alone with no family having ever existed, no friend having ever met you, money having no value, and work not being a staple of society, then what would you find important? I know, it's hard to imagine anything at first. But when the idea starts to sink in, then it's easy to imagine yourself living a carefree, rule-less life. Let's try and find somewhere in the middle. Would you mow your lawn every week in summer if someone didn't ask you to? Would you send greetings cards if it wasn't deemed socially normal? Would you swat a fly or squeal when you saw a spider on the kitchen floor if there had never been anyone around to suggest it? I don't think I would. If I could do anything, I'd let my grass grow long and wild, filling itself with bees, butterflies, snakes, and critters of all sorts. Dandelions, daisies, and forget-me-nots would reach my window sills.

When taking on a new belief system, we revisit pretty much everything about ourselves all over again.

Why am I doing this?
Who am I doing this for?
Does this make me happy?
Does this serve my purpose?

It is a shame that we live in a world where so much of our "choice" is either/or. We have so many wonderful opportunities, but what no one mentions as you are growing up is that you can do one or the other. In one life, there isn't enough time to do it all. Spirituality cannot change such things, but you can use it to help find what it is that is truly important to you, so that you can reprioritise your life and use the spare time you do have thoroughly and enjoy true divine happiness that you have created for yourself.

I began my journey to living my bliss after a long and severe battle with depression and anxiety that swamped me so deeply, I had no idea who I was and where I was going. When I decided I truly wanted to be happy, my only option was to look at my priorities. I had to shed the skin I had naively built in my childhood, the one that somewhat prepared me on the outside to look and act how I thought the world wanted me operate, and rediscover who it was that was underneath. I won't lie. I won't say it was easy. I won't pretend it happened overnight. All these years later, I won't claim that everyone understands. I had to address what it was that I wanted and stop giving all of my power to those things that I didn't want. This journey is ever-changing, ever-evolving, and ever so complex. However, I wake up every single day with the power to do exactly what I love to do.

I want you to ask yourself a series of questions. These questions may be very challenging for you to answer, so please come back time and time again to check in with your answers. Your answers need not be enormous or life-changing at first:

What do you consider, from your honest authentic core, to be most important to you? Deep inside your heart, what is it that you really want? What do you want to do and how do you want to go about doing it?

The hardest part about truly defining what is important to you is that we live in a society that has its own ideas about what is important and what is not. From birth, your mind has been penetrated with these ideas, concepts, and judgements of what is and what is not acceptable. Now you must break away from everything you have ever been taught, learned, heard, said, and thought. Many of those things will be true values for you. But how can you know until you address them all in detail?

When we manage to align our individual expression of life here on the third dimension with our core values and priorities, then it is hard for us to live unhappily any more. Once you have felt true happiness and learned how to create it for yourself, you refuse to give your power away at all costs. This is not selfishness, as society would have us believe, this is simply the difference between living and surviving.

It can feel very complicated when you are coming from a very busy, overwhelming, structured life to a point where you attempt to begin the journey of finding your true bliss. However, when you find the balance, life becomes so easy that the life of a child seems difficult in comparison.

A living being that can act out the values they possess is filled to the brim with pleasure and alignment to the universe or source energy.

Does this mean sad, uncomfortable things will never happen again? Of course not, but it does mean how you perceive and cope with them will differ greatly in your favour. Your happiness is born when you live and prioritise according to your values.

Happiness is not a constant state the same way depression is. There are pathways to depression and there are pathways to happiness. At any point down the road, you can check in with your internal compass and realise you may have gone the wrong way. And that's ok. You just take a detour to where you need to go.

Have you ever heard the term "let the chips fall where they may"? When you prioritise in accordance to your values and sense of belief, then a lot is going to change. People will see you differently and behave differently towards you, and they may not always be supportive. Human beings are very resistant to change, and when an outsider can see you growing spiritually, this can be threatening for them. You are moving forward without them, ascending on your journey and leaving them behind.

Some people will even go as far as to try and manipulate you or hold you back, although they may genuinely think they are doing what is best. It is of the utmost importance that when you decide to truly begin living by your values that you stay on course. Changing your life is easy, but trying not to question yourself when everyone around you looks on confused is very hard.

Eclectic Book of Shadows

My dear reader,

The following pages are laid out to use as a
practice Book of Shadows before you start your
very own. Here you can write down all the little
bits of information you find most interesting and
important. The majority of Wiccans start their
Book of Shadows with a book blessing, and so
I have written one for you with blank spaces for
you to fill in with your own
personal information.

I ,(Your Name)...
dedicate this book to be my sacred and divine
journal for the purpose of love, light and
Pick something you feel is most important

....

Though others may find my book of growth, desire, and spiritual discovery, their presence and touch will not compromise the vibrational frequency and intentions of the pages within.

Blessed by the Elements of Earth and Air, Fire and Water, I connect my book to nature and all that resides in its home.

I place my hand in the soil and onto my book to bless its pages with the power of the Earth.
I pass my incense over my book to bless its pages with the power of Air.

I pass a candle over my book to bless its pages with the power of Fire.
I sprinkle a drop of water over my book to bless its pages with the power of Water.

I bless my book with light and positivity and promise to never use it for harm or low-frequency agendas.

I bless my book with my heart and soul, with the powers of divine masculine and feminine to unite the world as one.

I bless this book for now and always with truth, with desire, and with passion.

I bless this book with all I have and now it becomes a part of me.

So mote it be.

The next addition to this Eclectic Book of Shadows is the Wiccan Rede, followed by many of the subjects in parts one and two of this book.

A Book of Shadows is also used as a diary to write down how you feel about your spiritual growth, thoughts, and desires. Any joys you feel, any pleasures, as well as any fears and anxiety.

This is also where witches record their spell work, with much of a witches first spells being trial and error, discovering what works for them as an individual and what they feel they like.

In short, your Book of Shadows can be used as a study guide, a journal, a confession, a gratitude list, an index of spells, and so much more.

Use the following pages as practice sheets so you can get everything perfect before you start your first Book of Shadows.

Eclectic Book of Shadows

Acknowledgements

As an avid reader, writing a book always seemed a little too far out of my reach. The amount of stories and guides I have created over the years is almost impossible to count, but they never made it any further than my external hard-drive. Mango Publishing saw something in me that gave me the chance to prove to myself I could do what I had always wanted, and I will be forever grateful for that opportunity and all of their hard work.

I suppose the majority of my thanks goes to my friends—without their years of listening to my thoughts and opinions, I would have nothing to write about at all. Arron, whom without I would never have cast my first circle. Stephanie, whom without I doubt I would understand my true power as a divine feminine being. And Aimi, who despite not coming from a Pagan path herself, is so used to my speeches that she now refers to the universe multiple times a day.

My Mother, Father, and Sister always openly supported my choice to follow my own spiritual path and religion. Not many witches are lucky enough to say their first trip to the beautiful spiritual town of Glastonbury was a family outing.

Lastly but certainly not least, I thank those who continue to support my work and my online presence, and work with me time and time again. I thank you all for being patient with me over the years as I discovered and continue to discover the way. I send such love and blessings to you all.

Author

There is a little witch in all of us, but quite a lot in Mandi See. The Spiritual teacher and counsellor started her business in 2012 to help guide the spiritual enthusiasts of the world to a place they felt comfortable, happy, and most importantly, at home. Since then, Mandi has become a certified crystal healer, reflexologist, Tarot reader, aura and chakra expert, life coach, and palm reader, to name a few. With a following of over 100,000 that spans the internet and her website, Mandi hopes to continue to inspire, impress, and promote self-healing and love.

Mango Publishing, established in 2014, publishes an eclectic list of books by diverse authors—both new and established voices—on topics ranging from business, personal growth, women's empowerment, LGBTQ studies, health, and spirituality to history, popular culture, time management, decluttering, lifestyle, mental wellness, aging, and sustainable living. We were recently named 2019 and 2020's #1 fastest-growing independent publisher by *Publishers Weekly*. Our success is driven by our main goal, which is to publish high-quality books that will entertain readers as well as make a positive difference in their lives.

Our readers are our most important resource; we value your input, suggestions, and ideas. We'd love to hear from you—after all, we are publishing books for you!

Please stay in touch with us and follow us at:

    Facebook: Mango Publishing
    Twitter: @MangoPublishing
    Instagram: @MangoPublishing
    LinkedIn: Mango Publishing
    Pinterest: Mango Publishing
    Newsletter: mangopublishinggroup.com/newsletter

Join us on Mango's journey to reinvent publishing, one book at a time.